"CJ McClanahan delivers a compa strategies. His common sense ana practical advice is packed with vivid examples. I rate this entertaining and inspirational read 'best of show.'"

— **Mickey Maurer, Author and Entrepreneur**

"This is a dynamite book. I'm one of the last people who would look to a book for guidance on living the life I imagine for myself. Yet Thrive is eminently readable and packed with great ideas and tools to do just that. If anyone has doubts that his or her life has the meaning and enrichment all of us aspire to have, then I would strongly encourage them to read and follow what CJ has compiled in Thrive."

— **Kevin Ober, Executive Director**
Indiana Republican State Committee

"Thrive is an excellent practical guide to better living written by a man who practices what he writes. Read it. Then live it! If you do you will find true success."

– **Dr. Greg P. Sipes, Clinical Psychologist**
Senior Partner, Indiana Health Group, Inc.
Founder, nextVoice, LLC

"Thrive is not your typical business book. CJ McClanahan is an author that "gets it" that we Americans live crazy busy lives, and he provides guidelines and real life examples to help us apply the lessons, all with a sense of humor and honesty that makes it hard to put down. Thrive is an insightful and relevant message to help business people not only create the success they desire, but enjoy the ride ... and live an extraordinary life."

— **Nicole Bickett, CEO**
Vision Bridge

"CJ McClanahan writes like he speaks—his enthusiasm for life comes through every page of this book! He's practical, witty, and wise. But don't be fooled. This book isn't like other books you've read about a life well-lived. As he puts it: 'books don't work, people do.' So, open the pages of this book and let his words go to work in your life. You'll be glad you did!"

— **The Rev. Dr. Steven J. Ebling**
New Hope Presbyterian Church, Fishers, Indiana

THRIVE

Seize your extraordinary life
with five simple strategies.

CJ McClanahan

Published & distributed by:

reach**more**
CJ McClanahan
10412 Allisonville Road, Suite 113
Fishers, IN 46038
www.goreachmore.com

in association with:

IBJ Book Publishing
41 E. Washington St., Suite 200
Indianapolis, IN 46204
www.ibjbp.com

ISBN 978-1-934922-33-0
Second Edition

Printed in the United States of America

To my mother.

Your courage, patience and love inspire me every day.

FOREWORD

Another self-help book? Can there really be anything new to say? Our modern era of easy publishing has led to a proliferation of "how to" self-help books. I've read dozens perhaps hundreds of these books. Some are helpful, few provide any new perspective and, most significantly, too often the credentials or credibility of the author is suspect. Of course the last consideration, credibility of the author, is the most important. Anyone can distill a set of principles into a system for life successes, but do they live it? Whenever you find an author who validates his or her thesis with their everyday life, then take interest in what they are saying. Read and reread his or her material.

CJ is a genuine, sincere, authentic man. He "walks the talk." I can offer no more profound recommendation of any book except that the author's "heart is in the right place." This is true with CJ. His heart is in the right place and he attempts to walk the talk every day in every way. This alone validates CJ's message and suggests this is an important read. But there's more!

While this book speaks of timeless principles and of sure-fired strategies for a better, more satisfying life it also notably speaks of a truth too often under emphasized or even ignored in our society - accountability. Accountability to God, spouse, family and friends and more: accountability to one's self. That's right, accountability to one's self. Without it, there is no accountability to God, spouse, family or friends. Accountability starts with personal reflection followed by a fearless personal inventory and then personal resolve to live better. After all, we really manage only one thing – ourselves.

Read CJ's book. Embrace his philosophy, the principles, of successful living. They will work! But not unless you are inspired. It is not principles but emotion that moves us to action. Be inspired by his life. Realize that if you will follow his lead and authentically live this thesis you will succeed. It's a sure-fired strategy to the life you've always wanted.

Dr. Greg Sipes
SEPTEMBER 2010

TABLE OF CONTENTS

CHAPTER 1
THE SELF IMPROVEMENT INDUSTRY

*"Self-improvement is the name of the game,
and your primary objective is to strengthen
yourself, not to destroy an opponent."*

– Maxwell Maltz
US plastic surgeon, motivational author,
and creator of the Psycho-Cybernetics

I know a guy named Bill who is a self-improvement junkie. He reads all the self-improvement books he can get his hands on, listens to tapes, and attends a wide array of seminars. Every time I see him, he spends the entire conversation passionately trying to convince me that he has just uncovered the key to unlimited passive income, perfect health, daily organization, conflict resolution, marketing, sales, or leadership.

I admire Bill's commitment to constant and never-ending self-improvement. No matter how much time and money he has spent on learning, he never stops looking for that next amazing breakthrough.

For example, a few years back, he read Robert Allen's *No Money Down*, and was convinced that he could flip houses on his lunch break and retire by the time he was twenty-eight years old. Next, he read *The E-Myth*, by Michael Gerber, the bestselling business book that inspired Bill to invest in an operations manual for his small business. Another of his favorites was *The 4-Hour Workweek*, by Timothy Ferriss, which convinced Bill that he should be able to run his business from a beach in Cancun. Unfortunately, after more than seven years of consistently filling his mind with the latest and greatest self-improvement information, Bill has yet to flip his first house; he lost his operations manual and hasn't even been to Cancun.

If you're reading this book, chances are that you know a person like Bill. Maybe you even recognize Bill every time you look in a mirror. You saw the cover of *Thrive*, liked the graphics, and thought, "This looks interesting. Maybe I've found a book that will help me reach my goals!"

While I appreciate the enthusiasm and believe that this book contains a very simple and powerful formula for success, I doubt it will be the end-all, be-all. (However, if it is, please tell all your friends!)

On that note, I want to let you in on a little secret about the self-improvement industry: there's nothing new to be written about self-improvement.

While visiting Borders® approximately three years ago, a book caught my eye titled, *The Magic of Thinking Big*, by David Schwartz. I thought, "Finally, a book that can help push me through to the next level and help me to think BIG!" This book had some fantastic insights, including the importance of believing in yourself, filling your environment with successful people, and a positive attitude.

It was a great book; in fact for the right person, I could see it being "life-changing" because it pointed out some simple and powerful advice that applies to everyone. However, for me, it was just a reinforcement of ideas and concepts I had read many times over. After reading the last page, I decided to flip to the copyright page and see when it was written. Shockingly, it was first published in 1959! At that very moment, I realized that these fundamental self-improvement principles have been around for more than fifty years. (Actually, quite a bit more–*Think and Grow Rich*, produced by one of the earliest writers to focus on self-help, Napoleon Hill, was published in 1937.)

For years, the self-improvement/goal setting/"get better quick" industry (my industry, by the way), has been repackaging the same ideas and concepts in the hope that someone will eventually find a combination of words on paper that will lead to a meaningful change in behavior.

Here's the interesting thing about self-improvement books, seminars, and audio programs: They don't work unless you work. These authors can provide you with a crystal-clear map, but it's your journey, not theirs. If you choose to ignore their teachings then you might win an award for reading the most books, but it's unlikely that you will change your behavior and achieve your dreams.

That's why I wrote this book.

I firmly believe that I have developed a simple plan for helping you achieve *your* extraordinary life. In addition, I have structured this 149-page lesson plan to ensure that you make a handful of behavioral changes along the way.

This is a journey, and, just like any other trip you have travelled in your life, it will be filled with some great stops, fantastic views, and interesting surprises. At other times, you will be frustrated and maybe even a little scared.

Whatever happens, remember, this journey is not a sprint. Our goal isn't to reach the finish line faster than anyone else. The purpose is to enjoy the scenery, while learning and developing a handful of habits that will open up the extraordinary life that is already all around you.

Let's go!

WHAT I REALLY WANT YOU TO REMEMBER...

Let's be honest: the minute you put down this book, you are going to switch to another activity that will bombard you with information; regardless of how compelling my book has been, you will forget most of what you have read. As a result, at the end of each chapter, I have provided you with a handful of key points that I really want you to remember. When you are trying to impress your friends with how smart you are, it is no longer necessary to go and re-read the entire book – just review the end of each chapter!

1. **It's Time to Just Do It**™ – It's all been written before. Most people know what it takes to be successful, they just don't do it. The key is to slow down and implement what you have learned.

2. **Enjoy the Journey** – Whatever you learn from this book or anything else in life, remember it is just a brief stop along a miraculous journey that is life. You will never know it all or get it all figured out. Instead of trying to sprint to a so-called "finish line", slow down and enjoy the journey.

CHAPTER 2
EXTRAORDINARY LIFE DEFINED

*"Success means having the courage,
the determination, and the will to become the
person you believe you were meant to be."*

– George Sheehan,
Andersen Consulting CEO, 1989 -1999

THE EXTRAORDINARY LIFE DEFINED

Shortly after I started my business in 2003, I undertook an exercise that had been recommended by many of my peers—I created a Dream Board.

A Dream Board is a 24" x 36" poster covered with pictures of all the stuff that you dream about. It is designed to help you visualize what it is that you want to achieve, acquire, and become. The reason the board is regarded as being so powerful is because most people are visual, and once your brain has a visual image of exactly what it is that you want to achieve, you can figure out how to get it done.

DREAM BOARD

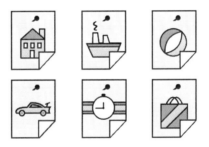

I completely agree with this theory, and as a result, in the fall of 2003, my wife and I visited the local bookstore and bought a dozen magazines filled with pictures of our dreams and went to work.

My pictures typically focused on "guy" stuff. I had a variety of luxury cars, a Rolex®, a big house in the mountains, a huge entertainment system, pictures of golf courses I wanted to play, a boat, and a wine cellar. I was going to be the MAN! My wife's was slightly different; she had jewelry (tons of it), exotic foods, and pictures of exotic travel locations.

We put them all together on one big board, stood back, and marveled at our creations. The next day, the artwork was hung in our home office (a.k.a., the basement).

Like any good self-improvement disciple, I looked at this board every day, closed my eyes and imagined what it would be like to drive that BMW®, wear that Rolex®, and drive my boat towards our summer home on the lake. It was going to be fantastic.

Over the next few months, I noticed that I was looking at the board less and less. I rarely closed my eyes and really visualized the car, the watch, and other luxury items. A year went by before my wife and I concluded that visualization didn't work, and the Dream Board made it into the garbage can.

I had to find another way to help me stay focused on my goals and dreams.

Maybe I needed to go and buy a fake Rolex® and wear it every day to truly understand the joy of having a luxury watch. Perhaps I needed to listen to a friend's recommendation and test drive a new BMW®, smelling the leather and feeling the experience of driving a fifty thousand dollar car. Maybe I could spend my weekends visiting open houses in extravagant neighborhoods in order to fulfill my yearning for a big house. After considering these alternatives, I decided that I needed to revisit my goals and dreams. Did I really want a luxury car, nice watch, and a huge house? Would having a boat next to a lake house make my life a living dream? I soon realized that the reason I was having trouble focusing on these items wasn't that visualization didn't work; my struggles were due to my focus on, and visualization of, the wrong things.

This brings us to the question that we all must ask ourselves: *How do you define your extraordinary life?* What is your purpose, and what are your goals and your dreams for an amazing future? This is *THE* question. *Nothing else matters* unless you give it some careful thought and consideration.

To illustrate this argument, consider the following hypothetical situation.

You are stranded in the middle of the ocean on a rubber raft with a set of oars and enough food and water to last for no more than two days. Approximately ten miles due north of your current location is a tiny island inhabited by a team of scientists studying the wildlife. These scientists have food, water, a phone, and transportation off the island. It will take you exactly two days to get there in your raft using the oars provided.

For the purpose of this example, you can't use the sun, the stars, or anything else to provide you with any direction.

A magic genie pops up a few feet in front of your raft and provides you with a choice. He tells you that he will grant you **one** of the following two items:

- A motor that will get you to the island within six hours
- A compass

Which item do you choose?

Unless you are a nerd and over-thinking the scenario, you will choose the compass. How much will a motor contribute if you have no idea where you are going? All you would do is drive all over an empty ocean until you ran out of food and water.

Let's consider a real life situation. Imagine that I am sitting in a room of successful business owners and executives, and I provide them with a choice:

- Make a commitment to regularly stop all activity and begin planning for the future with the entire senior management team.
- Work harder, stay later, and start more projects.

What do most of these busy executives choose?

That's right, they choose the second option. They operate under the assumption that carefully planning for the future is a luxury they don't have due to their demanding schedule. Never mind that they have no idea if all of this effort is getting them where they need to go.

As Dr. Steven Covey points out, you must "begin with the end in mind."[1] If you don't, you will continually mistake activity for achievement. This error will result in lots of effort (fifty-plus hour workweeks) that only brings you closer to someplace you don't want to be.

It's time to get out your compass and figure out how YOU define an extraordinary life.

Before we begin, understand that this is not going to be easy. It will require you to set aside all of your preconceived notions of success. For many of you, the process will result in the realization that you have been working towards the wrong goal for the majority of your professional career. This realization is often so frustrating that it results in the abandonment of the entire process.

Other people might struggle with this exercise because they don't believe they deserve an extraordinary life. Their parents worked sixty-plus hours a week, leaving little to no time for other things in their life, including family and friends. This continuous absence from the spouse and children's lives resulted in the family members feeling loneliness and neglect, as well as a loss of self-esteem. These people who experienced such neglect might feel selfish for wanting more than they currently have.

The majority of you will struggle with this process because you convinced yourself that you lack the skills necessary to achieve the extraordinary life. You feel you aren't smart enough, don't have the right education, or don't have the professional background. Those big dreams are for others, not you.

While it is extremely important that you understand why you behave the way you do (of which thousands of books have been written about this topic), that is not the focus of this journey. I'm not concerned about where you have been; I'm here to help you understand where you are going.

Understanding your extraordinary life requires more than just changing the background of your computer to a beautiful sunset on a tropical island; it requires you to give some careful thought to a handful of important questions. Your answers will help paint a compelling picture that will inspire you to make the changes necessary for achieving your dreams.

Before we begin answering these questions, remember that this is YOUR extraordinary life. Resist the urge to build a "Dream Board" based upon what you see on television or read in *People*® magazine. Your answers should be designed to inspire one person–you.

QUESTION #1
WHERE DO YOU LIVE?

I want you think about your perfect home. Is it in your current town or is it bigger? Does it have a swimming pool, a huge kitchen, or maybe even a guest house? Do you have multiple homes? Where are they located? How much time do you spend at each one?

As you go through this exercise, pay attention to the details. Your goal is to have a crystal-clear image; the more transparent the picture is in your mind, the easier it is for your brain to figure out how to achieve that image.

QUESTION #2

WITH WHOM DO YOU LIVE AND SPEND YOUR TIME?

I live in Indianapolis, and as I complete this book, our town and its inhabitants have just been through an awful winter with tons of snow and freezing cold temperatures. I hate winter. As a result, my answer to question one would never include Indianapolis, except for the fact that my answer to question two is more important to me than warm weather.

My family lives in Indianapolis, and my in-laws live three hours west in Illinois. As much as I would love to wake up every day and walk out on my patio greeted by sun and seventy-five degree weather, it is far more important that I get to spend quality time with my family. In addition, it is essential that my kids (ages four and seven) spend quality time with their family (not to mention the free babysitting we receive from their grandparents).

So, as you consider this question, keep in mind that your relationships are an important part of your life. In fact, a close friend of mine, Dr. Greg Sipes,[2] would argue that life is *only* about relationships. His belief, one with which I agree, is that no matter what you accumulate or achieve in life, it will mean absolutely nothing if you don't have meaningful relationships with the people close to you.

QUESTION #3

WHAT DO YOU DO PROFESSIONALLY?

Many people are tempted to answer this question by saying,

"Nothing; I don't have to work in my perfect life." Let me provide a little guidance on this question. I think it's okay to have a goal of not working in order to provide for yourself financially, but if you are reading this book, chances are good that you are a high achiever and will need to do something professionally or you will get bored.

So, ask yourself: What do you enjoy doing the most? What provides you with energy? What activities do you look forward to doing? What profession is best suited for your unique skills and abilities?

Speaking to a large crowd about an issue for which I have passion is the profession that best suits me. I look forward to every opportunity to inspire a group, and I enjoy watching the participants grasp a concept and become energized about the possibilities for improving their lives. I could do it all day long, seven days a week.

As you consider this question, keep in mind that it's okay if what you're passionate about is completely different than your current occupation. A meaningful journey rarely begins a few feet from the finish line.

QUESTION #4
HOW IS YOUR HEALTH?

Occasionally, when I look at myself in the mirror, I think it would be cool to look see a washboard stomach, chiseled biceps and broad shoulders. I quickly realize that I am six feet five inches tall, thin, and unlikely to ever have big muscles. I still work out five days per week because I realize that I can't enjoy my extraordinary life if I am not living a healthy lifestyle.

The reason this question concerning health is so important has nothing to do with how you look in a bathing suit; it lies in the fact that there is a direct connection between your well-being and your ability to achieve your goals. This connection has to do with the decisions you make each day. We tend to make better decisions when high energy levels and low stress levels are prevalent in our daily lives. Exercise and a healthy diet lower stress and increase your energy level throughout the day, which helps you make better decisions and keeps you on the path to your extraordinary life.

The best way to envision a healthy lifestyle is to consider the following questions: What is your ideal weight and body fat composition? How often do you exercise? Do you compete in athletic events, such as marathons and triathlons? What are the characteristics of your diet?

QUESTION #5
HOW DO YOU GIVE BACK TO YOUR COMMUNITY?

Over the past seven years, I have worked with hundreds of clients and have witnessed some amazing professional achievements, but I have yet to have a client who felt satisfied without giving back to others. In addition, our Creator has insisted that we do unto others as we would have them do unto us.[3]

Unfortunately, in today's society, most people are focused exclusively on the accumulation of accolades, wealth, and material possessions. We tell ourselves that we will begin giving back when our finances are in order and our kids have graduated from college, but soon after reaching these milestones we have replaced our desire to give back to others with the desire for new possessions that we "need" to acquire.

It never ends. That's why I am convinced that your extraordinary life must include giving back to others and making it a priority. Ask yourself, "Who needs my help? How can my unique talents and skills make a difference in the life of someone who is less fortunate?" We will talk more about the importance of giving back in Chapter 5. Until then, I would encourage you to visit *www.TheRule.org* and learn a little bit more about our foundation that is committed to helping successful business professionals understand the importance of giving back.

QUESTION #6

WHAT WILL YOUR FRIENDS AND FAMILY SAY ABOUT YOU AT YOUR FUNERAL?

Each time I take a client through this exercise I am tempted to have him or her answer this question first. I avoid doing this because it's valuable for each of us to design our vision for a perfect life and compare it to what we would hope is said about us at our funerals. Most will recognize a disconnection between what we hope to achieve and how we want to be remembered. For example, I have many clients characterize an extraordinary life with homes throughout the world, millions of dollars in the bank, and a great golf game. Yet, when I ask them to write their eulogy, all they really care about is that their family and friends recognize that my clients loved them and made their well-being a priority.

Therefore, it's likely that after you develop a clear understanding about what you want said at your funeral you might need to go back and revisit your answers to the previous five questions. That's perfectly normal; it's a natural part of the process.

THE FINISH LINE IS HERE

Now that you have a crystal-clear image of your amazing life filled with vivid details about where you will live, who you will spend your time with, what you will do for a living, how you will pay attention to your health, and how you will give back to others, I would like to add an important point.

As important as it is to complete this exercise and stay focused on these details, it is essential to realize an extremely important truth: You already have an extraordinary life.

That's right. It doesn't matter if you are in a dead-end job, if you are overweight, and if you have managed to screw up all of your closest relationships; you are exactly where you are supposed to be at this point in the journey.

I understand that this must sound like a complete contradiction to what we have just discussed, but there's an important reason why you must balance your journey towards a perfect life with a recognition that you are already there.

High-performing, driven professionals are never satisfied with the status quo, even if their current situation has the exact characteristics of the perfect life they once felt was unattainable. No matter how many achievements are conquered, the majority of people always want to attain more. This yearning is healthy and appropriate as long as the desire to achieve is balanced with an acknowledgment and appreciation of all that has been accomplished. It's imperative for you to count your blessings that appear along the journey.

Consider the following scenario: George, an eighty-year-old man who is lying in a hospital with just days to live, looks around the room and sees cards and flowers from family members, coworkers, and influential members of the community. After developing four different companies, being recognized locally and nationally as the most talented business person in his industry, travelling around the world, and out-earning and achieving more than all of his peers, George now feels empty and alone.

He quickly realizes that he never really enjoyed his life journey; he always looked for the next best thing. Every time he reached a goal, he immediately set a new milestone without taking a minute to celebrate his accomplishments. This realization leads him to ask the question, "Why did I work so hard if I was never going to enjoy any of my achievements?"

The journey is more important than the destination, and the best way to enjoy this voyage is by learning to balance an appreciation for your current circumstances with a healthy desire to push forward and achieve more. If you're like most, including me, this balancing act is not easy. I find it to be a daily challenge, and that's why I have developed a simple set of rules for achieving, living, and appreciating your extraordinary life.

WHAT I REALLY WANT YOU TO REMEMBER...

1. **Set Meaningful Goals** – Before you begin any journey, you need to determine your destination. If you don't have a clear picture of where you want your life to go, then it is unlikely that you will get anywhere. You may stay really busy, but it's unlikely that you will achieve the type of goals that are important to you.

2. **It's Your Life** – Resist the urge to create an extraordinary life that is characterized by the kinds of things that others think are important.

3. **You Can't Go Back in Time** – You should reflect and learn from your mistakes, but there is absolutely no value in dwelling on your past – it's over, and unless you have a time machine, you can't do anything about it.

4. **Start with the Basics** – Most people struggle to define their perfect life because they don't know where to begin. Here are the basics questions you should ask yourself to get the process underway:

   - Where do you live?
   - With whom do you live and spend your time?
   - What do you do professionally?
   - How is your health?
   - How do you give back to your community?
   - What would you like your family and friends to say about you at your funeral?

5. **You Already Have the Perfect Life** – No matter how hard you work, there will always be someone who has accomplished more. On that note, as you travel on your path towards the perfect life, it's important to realize that you already have it. If you don't grasp this key concept you will always be frustrated, no matter what you accomplish.

CHAPTER 3
INSANITY

"Insanity: doing the same thing over and over again and expecting different results."

Albert Einstein
Inventor and scientist

I already have all of the answers – and so do you.

If you never read another book as long as you live, you probably already know much of what it takes to achieve all of your goals and dreams. You already have most of the necessary information, strategies, and insights. You just forgot (and keep forgetting) everything you've learned. It's a common problem that affects busy professionals, stay-at-home moms, retirees, and everybody else.

Intellectually speaking, achieving your goals is simple. All you do is pick a goal, lay out a reasonable action plan, and execute.

Disciplining yourself to do what you know needs to be done is the extremely difficult puzzle piece. A great lesson doesn't mean a thing if you forget the key concepts and neglect to put them into practice. As Dr. Steven Covey, author of the bestselling *Seven Habits of Highly Successful People*, pointed out, "To know and not to do, is really not to know."[4]

For example, on many occasions, I find myself driving twenty to thirty miles over the speed limit while rushing to an appointment. Typically, the reason I am running behind is because I try to get one more thing accomplished before I leave the office. I get frustrated because I *know* that arriving at an appointment on time is far more important than sending one more e-mail.

Or do I really know?

You see, I would argue that if I really believed this truth (always leave plenty of travel time), then my behavior would reflect this belief.

Unfortunately, it doesn't. Intellectually speaking, I know exactly what to do, but I continually struggle to discipline myself and change my behavior. Dr. Covey would argue that I clearly don't know.

WHY DON'T WE CHANGE?

Assuming that you can relate to this type of frustration, why do we continue to behave in such a fashion that we know will lead to these unacceptable, yet completely predictable, results?

While there are many reasons that certainly vary by individual circumstance, I believe that there are three fundamental factors that can reasonably apply to every person and situation.

First, we must understand the role that pain has in our decision making. You continually repeat the same mistakes because the consequences of your actions aren't painful enough to get you to change. For example, the reason that many people continue to run late to meetings is that a simple apology, such as, "Sorry I was a few minutes late," is usually followed by a brief, "No problem."

Because there is no consequence (pain) with being late to the meeting, you have no incentive to change and show up to meetings on time.

Imagine how the following experience might affect your behavior: You own a small business that is looking for a breakthrough client. After nine months, hundreds of hours of work and three proposals, you have finally been granted the opportunity to meet with the key decision maker at one of the largest companies in your area. Closing this deal will nearly double your sales and allow you to pay down most of your credit line.

After a final review of the material with your vice president of sales, you leave for the meeting. At precisely 10:04 A.M., you arrive at your 10:00 A.M. appointment. The key decision maker, Brian, greets you in his conference room.

As you begin to pull materials out of your briefcase, Brian interrupts, looks you squarely in the eye and says, "We will not be able to meet today, Mr. McClanahan. I very much doubt that you will be able meet our needs in the future if you aren't able to show up to our first meeting on time."

With that, he stands and leaves the room.

Hopefully, the financial consequences of losing this deal, along with the complete shock you felt as Brian left the room, will be painful enough to get you to change your behavior. Hopefully, the next time you have an important meeting you will leave with plenty of time for travel because you have now learned that no last-minute detail in your office is an important as being on time to a meeting. We are likely to change when the consequences of our old behavior are extremely painful.

The second reason that we don't change our behavior is associated with our addiction to instant gratification. In today's fast-paced professional workplace, we rarely engage in an activity that doesn't deliver an immediate result. Each day we look at our "to-do" list and focus on those items that are easy to complete. These typically include such activities as responding to an e-mail, completing a quick analysis of a document, or solving a problem with a client/employee/prospect.

Seldom do we tackle issues that are difficult and are unlikely to lead a quick outcome. For example, when was the last time that you sat at your desk, turned off your e-mail program, and dedicated time towards your strategic plan for the next five years? You avoid working on this type of document because your brain can't rationalize working on a task that won't yield an immediate result when there are so many simple tasks that can be completed in minutes. Another example happens every year during the month of January at gyms all over the country. Hundreds of people flock to the weights, treadmills, and Stairmasters hoping to fulfill their New Year resolutions only to quit by the first week of February because they didn't instantaneously lose thirty pounds or get huge muscles.

The absolute best discussion of this phenomenon is found in Dr. Covey's bestselling book, *First Things First*. In this masterpiece, Dr. Covey argues that we are *addicted* to urgency. He makes a compelling argument that many professionals judge their productivity by their pace and accompanying stress level. In other words, as professionals, we allow our workdays to be filled with activities that are urgent but not necessarily important. This affects our ability and desire to modify our behavior because change is typically hard work, and this work almost rarely yields an immediate result.

For example, I have a client who allows circumstances to run his day. He arrives at the office on Monday morning with grand plans for tackling the week, only to have those plans go out the window by 8:15 A.M. when he checks his e-mail and faces his first few challenges of the day. Not only is his behavior highly unproductive, it is also extremely disruptive to his staff. For example, it's not uncommon that he will tell four or five of his direct reports to drop whatever they are working on and come to his office immediately to discuss an issue. Rarely is this urgent interruption important enough to drive all of their efforts to a grinding halt. After completing a little research into the nature of these ad hoc meetings, I quickly realized that they arose because the team members failed to communicate on a regular basis.

You don't need to be a highly paid advisor like myself to recognize that a regular weekly meeting with a set agenda would eliminate 90 percent of these interruptions. However, it took me more than nine months to make this weekly meeting a habit.

Why did it take so long to implement an extremely simple and obvious solution to a very painful problem? Because every week, when it was time for our meeting, another challenge erupted that provided my client with a more immediate result/response than a boring staff meeting. He actually loved the interruptions and would seek them out every time the staff meeting arose. Clearly, he was addicted to urgency.

Earlier in my career, I had the exact same addiction to urgency. As the director of operations for a light manufacturing and distribution facility, I realized that the best use of my time was sitting in my office with the door closed planning our purchasing and analyzing our expenses for the next several months. At the slightest hint of a problem in the warehouse I would drop everything and run out to address the issue, whether or not my help was absolutely necessary. Ninety percent of the time the problems I solved could have been handled by the warehouse staff, but I preferred seeing an immediate result to my efforts over sitting in my office and planning for activities that may not deliver satisfaction for weeks.

Another example of our addiction to urgency that applies to most Americans is dieting. Most people above the age of ten are completely clear about how to lose weight: eat healthy and exercise. At the most basic level, you must burn more calories than you consume on a daily basis. It's that simple. Having said that, a quick search on the word "diet" at *www.Amazon.com* returned more than four hundred thousand results! We know exactly how to lose weight, yet because these two simple guiding principles are difficult to accomplish and don't deliver an instant result, thousands of new diet books are published (and purchased) every single year. What makes this whole thing ridiculous is that the authors of these books know that we all understand exactly how to lose weight. As a result, they are in a constant, silly competition to come up with the title that promises the quickest weight loss with the least amount of effort (*Rock solid abs in 2 weeks and eat McDonalds® for every meal!*). They are aware that we will not change unless there appears to be instant gratification. Intellectually, no matter how much we realize that delaying gratification is important to change, we struggle with our addiction to urgency and this struggle keeps us from achieving our goals.

Finally, the third reason that we don't change our behavior is that we are awful at creating an emotional connection between the effort required to change and the reward for changing. In other words, you won't alter your behavior if you don't really care about the person you will become after the change.

For example, imagine that you are going to remodel your kitchen. You visit the local hardware store and pick up paint swatches, flooring samples, and kitchen remodeling magazines. One week later you have cut out dozens of pictures, picked the perfect colors, and have a distinct visual image of exactly what your new kitchen will look like.

You proceed to remodel your kitchen but run into a variety of issues and problems, causing cost overruns and delays. Despite what issues and delays occur, you get it done. In addition, you schedule a party the week it is completed so that everyone can come over and see the new creation.

Now, let's go back to the weight loss example and imagine that during the same week you visited the hardware store you joined your local gym with the goal of "getting healthy." Approximately six weeks and nine gym visits later, you conclude that you don't have time to exercise.

Why are you able to complete your kitchen project but not able to implement a successful exercise program? Because every time you stripped a piece of wallpaper or laid a floor tile, you held the picture of your beautiful kitchen in your mind. You developed a strong emotional (and visual) connection between the hard work and the goal/achievement.

At the gym you work out for an hour, sweat, look at yourself in the mirror and conclude, "This is probably as good as I'm ever going to look." There is absolutely no emotional connection; all your focus is on the hard work with little or no results.

KEEP IT SIMPLE

Understanding why change is so difficult is fairly intuitive and simple. We need to build a powerful emotional connection between the desired change in behavior (losing weight, leaving early for appointments) and the pain associated with not changing (losing your biggest prospect) or the pleasure associated with changing (a healthier body and mind). In addition, we need to see some results along the way or we will get distracted.

No kidding! I very much doubt that this is the first time you have come across this analysis. As much as I would like to take credit for a breakthrough in change management, thousands of books have taught these simple principles to millions of readers for decades.

Yet, we still don't change. And after speaking to thousands and coaching hundreds of professionals, I think I know why—we make it too complicated. In a world filled with a constant and never-ending stream of new information, our brain overanalyzes typical problems and challenges. Every day, we are bombarded with hundreds of solutions to our problems, each one providing a new tactic that promises great results. We hear these solutions on the radio, watch them on television, and receive instant messages via our e-mail and Facebook® accounts. As a result, we just can't believe that the solution can be simple. If it were, why are there so many options?

Take a simple challenge like becoming a better salesperson. Since the inception of commerce, great salespeople have known that success in sales is a simple math equation that has two variables – the number of prospects and conversion rate. If you increase the number of prospects contacted and improve your conversion rate, your sales will grow.

It really is that simple. However, the more information we have, the more we complicate this simple solution.

Here's a classic example of adding too much complexity to a challenge: I had a client with a team of seven salespeople who were all struggling to increase their sales. Immediately, I instilled a handful of simple practices (increase prospecting and follow a sales process) that I knew would lead to success if followed properly.

A few months later, my client, the CEO, came to me and

announced that he was ready to purchase a web-based tool built specifically for his industry that was designed to help a sales staff set appointments. This solution employed a new "cutting edge" technology. I told him that I supported the idea, but before we pulled the trigger I wanted to ask two quick questions: "How many members of our current team have hit their prospecting numbers?", and "How many have implemented the sales process we rolled out?"

The answer to both questions was a resounding, "None."

Moments later, we both agreed that it made little sense to add a new approach to a sales team that had yet to prove that they could handle the current initiatives.

Does this scenario sound familiar? How many times have you quit the existing approach after reading an article or blog or after attending a seminar that promised quicker and easier results?

Our desire to find a quick and easy answer including an immediate result causes us to cover up simple solutions with layers of complexity. Because we just can't imagine that the simple answer is going to work and we have access to endless solutions, we ignore the obvious answer that is usually right in front of us. The challenge reminds me of a local Mexican restaurant that has great burritos. These burritos have just the right amount of cheese and chicken, and they have the perfect tortilla. Every time I eat there though, I am enamored by the fifty-seven choices at the hot sauce bar. Moments after I have received my PERFECT burrito, I have smothered it with eleven different flavors.

Just like I need to stick with the plain burrito, you need to simplify your tactical approach to addressing your challenges. Lay out a basic plan for reaching your goals, and unless you begin to fail miserably, stick with your plan. Resist the urge to make any major modifications to the approach if (when) you don't see an immediate result.

Before you begin to put the "simplicity" theory into practice, remember that it is counterintuitive to everything you hear in modern society. In our culture we are told that if our cell phones don't allow us to surf the Internet, listen to music, mow our lawns, and locate a Thai restaurant all while conversing with others, it is deemed "old-fashioned" and needs to be upgraded. We are all tempted everyday (virtually every hour) to believe that we aren't doing enough to reach our goals. Most magazine articles we read and Internet sites we visit promise quicker and better results if simple adjustments are made to our plans and *just one more* wrinkle is added to the process.

One of the fundamental lessons I want you to learn in this book is that you should resist the urge to change everything all the time. It's not your typical "self-help" read. Sometimes we need to slow down to speed up.

WHY ONLY FIVE?

In 2005, Jack Canfield authored *The Success Principles.* Since then, I have read the book (or listened on compact disc) many times and have given away more than 150 copies. In addition, I have an autographed copy of the first page sitting on my bookshelf—it is that important to me.

The reason I like the book so much is that Canfield essentially came out and admitted that we already know the greatest learning principles; they have been written about in dozens of books for decades. Canfield took sixty-four of these concepts and condensed them into comprehensible, extremely powerful chapters. This book is a common sense approach to life with straightforward lessons that can be applied by anyone. It is not uncommon for one of my clients to admit that *The Success Principles* has absolutely changed his or her life, and I always recommend it as one of the most important books I have ever read.

As I began to collect my thoughts for this book, I had grand visions of changing lives the way Canfield had changed mine and those of my clients. In doing so, I realized that what I liked so much about his approach was its simplicity. Although his approach was simple, it still represented sixty-four separate and unique concepts. In addition, if you truly implemented his teachings into your life, it would result in the development of sixty-four new habits. My experience over the last seven years has taught me that developing a new habit is difficult and can take months.

At this point in my reasoning I realized that in order to help the average individual make a meaningful change in their life, I had to make it easy. I had to come up with a formula, concept, theory, or set of rules that would be simple to grasp and could apply to anyone. In addition, these rules had to help the reader make meaningful changes in his or her behavior on a daily basis. The first thing I did was agree to a number and told myself that regardless of the great ideas or success principles that existed in the world, I had to limit the number to no more than five. Any more than five would result in the average reader losing focus and interest.

Narrowing hundreds of extremely helpful, wise, and powerful self-improvement principles down to five was not an easy task; some of my absolute all-time personal favorites had to be eliminated. I had to put together a list that I felt confident would make the greatest impact in the lives of others. Here is the finalized list (drum roll please):

1. Exceed Expectations
2. Be Grateful
3. Improve Every Day
4. Live in the Moment
5. Choose Your Future

Now, please note that by placing these five together I am not suggesting that the others (set powerful goals, plan your day, etc.)

aren't important. I am saying that I am certain that you can reach just about any goal by focusing solely on these five principles.

Sit back, relax, and prepare yourself to enjoy a simple approach to living your extraordinary life.

WHAT I REALLY WANT YOU TO REMEMBER...

1. **We Are All a Little Crazy** – Most people know exactly what they need to do to reach their goals. However, because we are all a little nuts, we continue the same behavior and expect different results.

2. **Change is Hard** – Intellectually speaking, changing a behavior is simple; actually changing that behavior is hard. There are three simple reasons why people don't change:

   - The pain associated with the current behavior isn't strong enough.
   - We only change behavior when there is instant gratification.
   - It's difficult to make an emotional connection with the possible rewards for change.

3. **KISS** – Most people make change really, really complex. If you want to change a habit, you need to Keep It Simple Stupid.

4. **Five** – I believe so strongly in keeping it simple that I have chosen five simple habits that will help you to achieve your extraordinary life:

   - *Exceed Expectations*
   - *Be Grateful*
   - *Improve Every Day*
   - *Live in the Moment*
   - *Choose Your Future*

CHAPTER 4
EXCEED EXPECTATIONS

*"High achievement always takes place
in the framework of high expectation."*

Charles F. Kettering,
Inventor and holder of one hundred forty patents

My wife Nicole and I just celebrated our tenth wedding anniversary. Over that ten-year period I have learned many, many things about how to be a better husband and a person. Like most men, I entered into this relationship believing that I had everything figured out and had very little room for improvement.

It turns out, I was wrong. To this very day, I am amazed how much I have yet to learn about improving my relationship with the most important person in the world to me. You would think that after ten years I should have encountered every challenge or situation and written an operations manual about how to be the perfect husband, but I often think I have yet to understand the first chapter.

I have learned a few things, and I have found that these important lessons apply to almost every other relationship that I have in my life, both personally and professionally. The most important lesson that I have learned about marriage and Nicole is that she doesn't expect me to be perfect. She recognizes my tendency to ignore the details and occasionally forget my wallet or phone at home. She knows that I am not exactly the most romantic individual you will ever meet and that it is highly unlikely I will provide any major surprises at birthdays or on our anniversary. That's just me.

When you ask Nicole what frustrates her most about my behavior, she will almost always tell you the same thing: She will point out that it's not the mistakes I make but the poor job I do in managing her expectations. For example, if I tell Nicole that I am going to be home at 6 P.M., she expects me home at 6 P.M. When I roll in at 6:15 P.M., she is not happy at all. Inevitably, I usually make the following type of comment, "I'm only fifteen minutes late. What's the big deal?" Nicole will argue that she doesn't care about when I get home; what upsets her is that I set an expectation of 6 P.M. and didn't meet that expectation. She craves predictability.

WHY ARE EXPECTATIONS SO IMPORTANT?

You know who has an intense desire to have you do exactly what you promise? Just about everyone, including your prospects, clients, friends, employees, and coworkers. From the minute you open your eyes in the morning until you have your final thought before drifting off to sleep, your life is filled with expectations. Some of these are met, others are exceeded, and many are missed completely.

Consider your typical day: you wake up in the morning and turn on the shower, expecting the water to be hot after running for a few minutes. What if the water only gets warm? In 90 percent of the world a warm shower would be a welcome luxury on a weekly basis, much less every day. However, because you were expecting piping hot water, you leave the shower disappointed. Your expectations have caused you to view an otherwise acceptable situation in a negative light.

As soon as you arrive at work, you walk into the break room to get a cup of coffee and realize that all they have is decaf. You begin to hyperventilate and wonder how you will ever make it through the morning without a jolt of coffee. Imagine if the office manager had alerted you in advance that they would no longer serve caffeinated coffee; would you be able to adjust, or would you resign your position? Of course, you would figure out how to get through the morning without coffee, or you may even decide to pick up your own on the way in to the office.

Later in the day, your e-mail server goes down, and it appears that you won't be able to send or receive e-mails until the next morning. Grabbing the paper bag you used earlier that morning during the coffee incident, you proceed to practice breathing exercises and begin to fret that every single one of your clients and prospects will move to your competition because of the inability to correspond with you for three hours. What if you knew twenty-four hours in advance that the Internet was going to be down for the afternoon? As with the coffee, you would adjust and fill your afternoon with activities unrelated to e-mail (and yes, those do still exist).

At the end of the long day, you walk into the house and slump into your favorite chair, happy to be home and away from the frustrations at the office. After dinner, you sit in front of the television eagerly waiting to catch the latest episode of your favorite show, *The Office*. For the first time since you woke up at 6 A.M., you feel completely relaxed. Then it happens; a few seconds into *The Office*, you realize that it is a re-run and NOT a new episode. Instead of enjoying thirty minutes of mindless humor, you are now forced to search through dozens of channels to find something to occupy your mind until you are ready to fall asleep. The only thing that pacifies you is that tomorrow will be a new day.

Looking back, did you really have that bad of a day? The shower wasn't hot, but it was warm. You were still able to get coffee and the e-mail was only down for one afternoon. And, even though *The Office* wasn't a new episode, you still had many other channels from which you could choose. The reason this day seemed so terrible wasn't that the circumstances were that bad, it's because these circumstances didn't match your expectations.

The more I learn about success, the more I recognize the importance of understanding and exceeding expectations. There are three reasons this is so important. First, the achievement of any goal can rarely be accomplished on your own; it requires you to build valuable relationships with other people, including your family, coworkers, employees, prospects, customers, friends, and neighbors. For example, if you own a business and want to double your sales, you will need a great staff to help you get there. If you are trying to lose weight, you would benefit from the support of your family and the assistance of a personal trainer. If you are writing a book, a good editor, or book "coach" as I call her, is absolutely critical to your success. The problem in building these relationships is that we are selfish. As soon as we begin to interact with someone we need to help us achieve our goal (employee, vendor, coworker, etc.) our brain immediately shifts into, "What can you do for me?" mode. Unfortunately, the other person is usually in the same mode, often resulting in poor communication, unmet objectives, and frustration. Before a meaningful relationship can be fostered, you need to develop a crystal-clear understanding of what the other person's unique expectations are for your relationship.

The second reason that exceeding the expectations of others is important is because, as my good friend Dr. Greg Sipes points out, life is *only* about relationships. As you begin to achieve some truly amazing goals in your life, you will soon recognize that the acquisition of wealth or material positions rarely leads to contentment. Similarly, it is unlikely that you will experience complete satisfaction from the attainment of fame. If you have any doubt, consider the trials of Tiger Woods, the thirty-year-old golf star who is the most recognized athlete in the world and worth a billion dollars. In order to lead a truly extraordinary life, you need to build and maintain significant relationships with those people in the world who mean the most to you. It's impossible to build these relationships if you don't take the time to understand their expectations.

If you have any doubt about the importance of building these important bonds, revisit the final question we discussed in our discussion of the perfect life. What would you want your family and friends say about you at your funeral? When I ask my clients and audiences to consider this situation, I never hear people say, "I would hope that it would be a business acquaintance who would focus on how much money I earned, awards I received, and sales I generated." Normally, when faced with this question, most suggest that they would like to hear from their family and closest friends. In addition, they envision that these people would use words and phrases like caring, loving, good listener, dependable, and fun. When all is said and done, the old cliché is true; life is only about how you have exceeded the expectations of those whom you love.

To recap, I believe that understanding and exceeding expectations are important because you need to interact with others in order to achieve your goals. Ultimately, your success will be directly related to your most valuable relationships. Striving to exceed expectations will help you measure your progress. Think about the last few times you struggled to build a positive bond with someone else. Typically, it's not because you didn't try; in fact, chances are that the more difficult the relationship became, the harder you worked at it. At some point you threw up your hands, exasperated, and wondered if anything would work.

The root of your frustration lies in your inability to determine if you are making any progress. The only way to overcome this aggravation is to clearly understand the expectations of the person with whom you are struggling. As soon as you appreciate these expectations, you will understand how to modify your behavior to meet and exceed them. In addition, this information is helpful because there are times that you will be unable to meet someone's expectations. Isn't it better to know that upfront from the person before you put in all the time and effort?

Early in my career, I coached a small business owner in the construction industry. After six months of coaching, I recognized that we weren't making much progress. I asked the client his opinion; he agreed and added that I hadn't met any of his expectations since we began. With my tail between my legs, I scheduled a meeting and asked him if he could detail exactly what he expected out of me as his coach during the next ninety days. This roadmap helped me to measure our progress every quarter for the next year. I quickly implemented this process with each of my clients and realized greater success with each one. The best part of this improvement was that we were able to quantify our improvement along the way.

The first of the five keys for building your extraordinary life is to always exceed expectations; your ability to achieve this amazing life will be heavily influenced by your capacity to develop and maintain meaningful relationships with others, both personally and professionally.

Now that we understand why exceeding expectations is so important, let's address whose expectations we need to exceed.

AUDIENCE FOR EXCEEDING EXPECTATIONS

One might ask the question, "Whose expectations should I focus on exceeding?" The answer is simple and straightforward: you should aim to exceed the expectations of everyone you come into contact with throughout your day, week, month, and year. That's right, I said everyone. Most people respond to this advice by arguing that it's impossible to exceed everyone's expectations all the time, but I didn't say it was going to be easy. If you're truly interested in living your extraordinary life you need to focus on asking yourself, "What does this person expect out of this interaction?" every time you pick up the phone, respond to an email, or greet a stranger.

I understand that it's easy to motivate yourself to exceed the expectations of your biggest client. On more than one occasion, I have "dropped everything" at the call or e-mail of our largest customer. I understand that if I don't meet their needs immediately, I run the risk of losing a large piece of revenue. Most people are very good at exceeding the expectations of their largest prospects because when sales are involved, exceeding expectations becomes second nature. However, if you only exceed expatiations when big money is on the line, you will miss out on the opportunity to develop the life-changing habit of exceeding everyone's expectations.

Here's a partial list of the people whose expectations I'd advise you to exceed, including an explanation of why I feel they're important. This breakdown should help you to see the importance of treating everyone like they were significant enough to deserve your respect and effort.

PROFESSIONAL	WHY SHOULD I EXCEED THEIR EXPECTATIONS?
Largest client	Obviously, the client who generates the most revenue should have a significant amount of your time and attention.
Smallest client	This client may one day become your largest customer or might have a relationship with your next big client.
Largest prospect	If you ever want a "largest client", you need to start somewhere.
Smallest prospect	See #2 and insert the word "prospect" where you see client.
Past customer	These people could come back one day and have a strong ability to influence future prospects, both positively and negatively, because they have previously used your product/ service.
Supervisor/ manager	If you are at all interested in getting a raise or a promotion, you need to be crystal-clear about what your boss expects from you and then develop a plan to exceed those expectations.
Employees	Your success is directly related to your ability to get those who work for you to perform at a high level. People work harder for leaders that consistently exceed expectations.
Co-workers	Influencing members of your team is a critical component to success in the workplace. These individuals appreciate their colleagues who exceed expectations.
Vendors	In addition to setting expectations, it's important that you understand what your vendors need from you in order to get the most out of their products and services.
Strategic relationships	There are important individuals in your industry who have the ability to help you succeed. If you want to maximize this influence, you need to understand what they expect from you in return and then deliver that, plus more.
Potential employers	You never know when it may be time to move on to another opportunity. Take time to develop relationships outside of your current employer.

PERSONAL	WHY EXCEED THEIR EXPECTATIONS?
Spouse	This is your life partner and arguably the most important living person in the world to you. Understanding and exceeding his or her expectations is a lifelong journey.
Children	Psychology 101 teaches us that parents have the most influence over the personalities our children will eventually develop. You don't need a Ph.D. to realize that setting and exceeding expectations throughout their childhood is helpful.
Parents	For many of us, there are no people in this world who love us as much as our parents. They deserve our respect and best efforts.
Siblings	It turns out that blood is truly thicker than water and your brothers and sisters probably make the short list of people you turn to in a crisis.
Close friends	Most of us have a handful of close personal friends with whom we share our deepest ambitions and fears. Keep them close by understanding their ambitions and deepest fears.
Other friends	These are people with whom you have a casual acquaintance. These peripheral relationships add a layer of relationships to your life.
Neighbors	You may see these people frequently, and for many of you, they will become close friends. A close-knit support group in the neighborhood is helpful in many different ways. (In addition, you will need to borrow something someday!)
Teachers	If you have kids, chances are that these individuals will play an enormous role in their development. Instead of being the parent who complains all the time, be supportive and get to know them.
Coaches	If your kids play sports, their coaches will help them to learn important skills (teamwork, fair play, shooting the ball, catching, etc.). They are typically volunteers and really appreciate the parent who goes out of their way to help.
Pastor	This is by far the hardest job in the world. Your pastor is underpaid, overworked and receives tons of complaints every week (the music was too soft/loud during the service, the childcare room was messy, the sermon focused too much on money, etc.). He or she desperately needs your support, and chances are, you will eventually need his or her support.
Strangers	This includes anyone you come in contact with, including a waiter, someone in the elevator, a checkout person at the mall, etc. Consider how much of a difference you could make in his or her life if you took the time to exceed his or her expectations.

Hopefully, you have a clear understanding of why it is important to focus on exceeding the expectations of everyone in your life. Don't all of these people deserve your full attention? Can you imagine how much more satisfying your life would be if instead of concentrating on what you expected from every relationship, you focused on what the other person expected? Do you know anyone who lives this way today? I rarely meet someone who can respond to that question with a name off the top of his or her head. What if you were that person?

Before we move on, let me be clear that I understand that you can't weigh the importance of everyone's expectations equally. In other words, I don't expect you to begin counseling sessions with the checkout person at the dry cleaner so that you can deepen your relationship. You need to determine how you allocate your time, energy, and focus. If this is challenging for you, then I would refer back to my question about your funeral. When all is said and done, who are the most important people in your life? Once you are clear about the answer to that question, you will be clear about how to distribute your resources. Pay very special attention to your answer and review it regularly. I know many successful business people who have spent all of their time exceeding the expectations of those in their professional life while ignoring the needs of their family and friends. As Dr. Sipes says, relationships are the only thing.

UNDERSTANDING EXPECTATIONS

Okay, now that we understand why expectations are important and whose expectations we need to exceed, it's time to discuss the process for understanding expectations. In theory, this is a fundamentally simple process. You basically ask the other person the following type of questions:

- *Employees* – "Fast forward twelve months, and imagine that your spouse just asked you to describe your boss. You tell him or her that I was the best leader you ever had. You continued by saying that I was paying you fairly, helping you to develop an amazing set of skills, and doing a great job of growing the business. What would I need to do to earn that response?"
- *Supervisor* – "What would I need to do during the next twelve months to earn a significant raise, a promotion, and your respect?"
- *Prospect* – "What do you need to hear about my product and service to conclude that we are a great fit for your company?
- *Customer* – "Imagine that you are at a conference with your peers. They ask about your satisfaction with our company, and you tell them that you would highly recommend using our services. What would we need to do to earn that recommendation?"
- *Family* – "What can I do to make this experience (weekend/evening/vacation) absolutely perfect for you?"

You get the idea. The best way to determine what someone expects from you is to ask him or her to imagine that your interaction has gone perfectly and follow up with, "What made it great?" Keep in mind that you will rarely receive a clear answer from people because typically they don't even know what they should expect from the communication. When someone gives you a vague answer, you may need to help him or her think it through. For example, imagine that your company provides professional services (attorney, accountant, engineer, etc.) and you ask your largest customer what it would take to earn a great referral. If he or she struggles to provide you with any concrete details, you might suggest that the perfect provider would respond quickly, communicate clearly, and deliver exceptional results on a regular basis.

As simple and straightforward as this appears, few people do it effectively because we tend to focus on our own expectations. It is our nature to assume that everyone would expect the same thing that we would if they were placed in the same situation. For example, early in my career I assumed that all of my clients wanted a mass of information concerning concepts that could improve their businesses. Consequently, every coaching session was filled with spreadsheets, PowerPoint presentations, and research I had prepared since our last meeting. I continued to do this, even after my clients informed me that I was giving them too much information. They begged me to focus on the basics (a.k.a., setting my expectations). I continued with the same approach; I couldn't imagine that anyone could find value without reams of data.

Luckily, I came to a realization—no matter how hard I tried, I couldn't get my clients to agree to my expectations through sheer force, and I changed my approach. Unfortunately, many of you have the same problem, which results in a lot of effort but few satisfied customers, employees, coworkers, family, or friends. You need to change your approach and recognize that it's not all about you. If you are interested in becoming a master at understanding expectations, focus on carefully listening to others and empathizing with their viewpoint. In other words, take time to truly understand their perspective before you say a word, send an email or promise a document. This is extremely hard for most overachievers who like to control every situation. Nevertheless, you need to become a better listener if you expect to really understand expectations.

SETTING EXPECTATIONS

Understanding expectations is just the beginning, not the end. Once you recognize what another individual expects from you in terms of delivering results, you need to decide if you have the capability or the desire to meet their expectations. For example, you may realize that a great prospect expects you to provide a service that is well outside of the competency of your company; maybe a customer wants you to expand into a new area that you know won't be very profitable for you in the long-term. In these circumstances, it's time for you to set, or reset, expectations.

Setting expectations provides you with an opportunity to make it easier to exceed those expectations in the future. Far too often, we allow other people to develop a set of expectations that are completely unrealistic. Many times, we don't even realize that they have these impractical hopes. Case in point, I have had many remodeling contractors as clients throughout my career. Inevitably, each time they land a new bathroom or kitchen project, they run into problems because their clients don't understand the realities of remodeling homes. The client is surprised when dust collects throughout the house; the project is delayed or over budget. As a result, no matter how much they like the finished product, the engagement doesn't end well and the client rarely refers the contractor.

This type of situation can be avoided if we take the time to set clear expectations throughout our interactions with others. For instance, every time I work with a remodeling contractor I advise them, as soon as the contract is signed, to inform the homeowner that the house will likely be messy during the project, delays will most likely occur, and any changes made by the homeowner will result in an increase in price. When the contractor keeps the house cleaner than expected, gets it done closer to the original due date than expected, or sticks to the original estimate, the client is thrilled and provides tons of referrals.

You don't just set expectations when you are beginning a big project. They need to be set and reset circumstantially throughout the day in both your personal and professional life. Professionally, you have many interactions during your work day that would go much better if others knew what to expect. For example, if I think there is even the slightest chance that I might be a few minutes late to a meeting, I call in advance and apologize. That way, the other person is completely okay if I walk into a 10 A.M. meeting at 10:02 A.M. Personally, the same rules apply. If you absolutely have to take a work call in the evening, make sure to tell your kids as soon as you get home that your playtime will likely be interrupted for a few minutes. They should be all right with the interruption if they know it is coming.

Expectations need to be set and reset if you have any hopes of exceeding them.

EXCEED EXPECTATIONS

Here's the interesting part of this first key for living your extraordinary life. After you have put in all of the time and effort in identifying the right people (remember, it includes almost everyone) and understanding or setting their expectations, exceeding these expectations should be easy. Think about it: if you know exactly what it's going to take to make someone happy, and you have reset these expectations to ensure that they are within your capability and desire, all you need to do is execute. It's that simple.

Imagine for a minute that you are working on closing a huge prospect; this opportunity will help you to exceed your quota by 50 percent. After a round of meetings your client has indicated that if you are able to meet their timeframe, deliver all of the requirements detailed in their RFP, illustrate your ability to correspond effectively throughout the project, and hit their price, the deal is yours. All you need to do is to execute.

As soon as you land this client, you immediately reset expectations with their leadership team and develop a crystal-clear understanding of exactly what you need to deliver during the next twelve months to receive a strong testimonial. Once you have all of this information, carrying out the plan is the only thing that remains.

Personally, this can be a little more challenging. Unlike a client or prospect who may agree to put his or her expectations in writing, it's unlikely (in addition to being impractical and unromantic) that you will be able to get your spouse to go along with this plan. Believe me, I know; I have tried. On more than one occasion, I have made the following statement to my wife, "Just so I am clear, if I take the kids to the park, clean the garage, and mow the lawn, I will have exceeded your expectations of me for this Sunday?" I am not kidding; I actually talk that way sometimes. When I do, my wife, Nicole, responds with a terse, "I'm not one of your clients, and this isn't the office."

In your dealings with friends or family you need to be

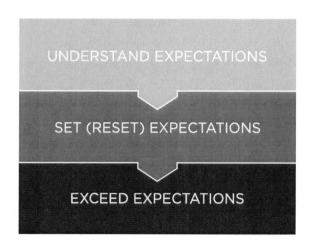

prepared for a little trial and error. Even Dr. Phil struggles to figure out what others are expecting from time to time, and you will too. Don't get frustrated when your kids don't give you an enthusiastic, "Hooray!" when you announce the summer vacation, or if your spouse is unhappy with the birthday gift you gave them. Even more difficult are your friends and distant family members; because you have less time with them, exceeding their expectations may at times seem impossible.

No matter how hard it seems, keep at it. Be the one person you know who puts the needs of others before himself or herself in an unselfish attempt to exceed expectations. This pursuit will result in a bigger bottom line, improved relations at home, and a great sense of satisfaction in all that you do. It's a simple 3 step process.

KEEPING TRACK

In addition to helping you grow your business and improve your personal relationships, there is another equally important reason to exceed expectations at all times: it helps you to measure your progress and learn from your mistakes.

Consider the last time you lost a sale. If you're like most sales people, you will cross the prospect off your list, assume your price was too high, and consider the entire effort a big waste of time. However, if you took the time to really understand and exceed his or her expectations, then losing the deal can provide you with an opportunity to improve. If you lost, then one of two things happened; you either didn't understand his or her expectations, or you failed to surpass them effectively. Either way, if you carefully analyze the transaction, you should be able to identify a lesson that will help you close a similar deal in the future.

This type of measurement is also important because you will often find it necessary to remind someone else of his or her original expectations. Most people are highly emotional and make their decisions based on how they feel, not from a review of the data. For example, when was the last time you asked a manager for a raise only to be told that you hadn't achieved enough to earn an increase in pay? Imagine how different this situation would play out if you have a detailed set of expectations that you have clearly exceeded during the past year. When talking with your client about a fee increase, would the conversation differ if you have carefully documented a simple set of agreed upon expectations?

Even at home, keeping track of your progress can help. When you screw up (which you will) and someone gets upset at your behavior, it's extremely valuable to be able to evaluate the situation based upon the expectations of the other person. Have you ever gotten frustrated with family members if they react poorly in a situation for (what appears to be) no good reason whatsoever? Consider my example from the beginning of this chapter; after I took the time to really understand Nicole's expectations, I realized why she got so upset when I returned home fifteen minutes late. Now I am careful to give myself plenty of time to ensure that I am always home by the time I indicated.

In each of these situations, you can't ever hope to improve your life personally or professionally if you don't quantify your progress because you can't improve upon something that you don't measure. The only way to measure your progress is to develop a baseline or a starting point; the best strategy for developing this basis with others is to begin with an agreed upon set of expectations.

WHAT I REALLY WANT YOU TO REMEMBER...

1. **Expectations are Everything** – In a word full of overachievers trying to outdo each other, it's more important than ever to understand what someone expects before you put in too much effort trying to please them.

2. **Start with Everyone** – Most people pick and choose whose expectations that try and exceed. Unfortunately, they tend to focus exclusively on their professional lives. Your extraordinary life isn't only filled with your boss and customers; you need to exceed everyone's expectations.

3. **Seek First to Understand** – Just as Dr. Covey advised in his bestselling book, *The Seven Habits of Highly Successful People*, before we can exceed expectations, we need to understand what they are and "seek first to understand before being understood."

4. **Set the Bar** – While it is important to understand expectations, sometimes it's equally important to set these expectations so that others don't set them too high.

5. **Clear the Bar** – Once the expectations are clear, the hard work begins. You need to constantly and consistently work at exceeding the expectations of others all the time.

6. **Measure the Results** – It doesn't matter if you think you are exceeding expectations; the opinions of others are what matters. You need to find out how you are doing and track your progress.

CHAPTER 5
GRATITUDE

"Gratitude unlocks the fullness of life. It turns what we have into enough, and more. It turns denial into acceptance, chaos to order, confusion to clarity. It can turn a meal into a feast, a house into a home, a stranger into a friend. Gratitude makes sense of our past, brings peace for today, and creates a vision for tomorrow."

Melody Beattie
Author of the bestseller, *Codependent No More*

A few hundred miles southeast of Miami, Florida there is a tiny island nation with more than nine million inhabitants. Although it takes a plane less than an hour to travel to this country from the high rise condominiums that stretch across South Beach, it might as well be on the other side of the globe. Haiti is as different from Miami as day is from night, or as black is from white.

Haiti is the poorest nation in the Western Hemisphere, and more than 80 percent of its population is unemployed. These people live on less than a dollar a day, and about 60 percent of the population lives in abject poverty. Less than 20 percent of the Haitians over the age of fifteen can read or write, and more than 75 percent of the children don't attend school.[5] Most of the Haitians live in the slums with little or no infrastructure. Only 30 percent have access to sanitation, with just slightly more than 50 percent having access to clean water.[6]

It's hard to believe that just a few hundred miles from the sunny shores of Miami (where a 1,000 sq. ft. condo lists for more than five hundred thousand dollars), there is a nation full of people struggling to find enough food to eat, water to drink, and/or a place to sleep.

As bad as the socioeconomic situation was for the Haitians, it became much worse for them less than two weeks into the New Year. On Tuesday, January 12, 2010, a catastrophic magnitude 7.0 earthquake hit Haiti, with the epicenter just sixteen miles west of Port au Prince, the nation's capital. Nearly two weeks later, the Haitian government reported that two hundred and thirty thousand people died, three hundred thousand were injured, and more than a million became homeless.

Growing up in a middle class neighborhood for my entire life I find it impossible to imagine what it would be like to grow up in a place like Haiti, much less suffer through one of the worst human tragedies that the world has ever seen. I can't get my arms around the concept of living in filth and not having access to clean water, a place to live, or a healthy diet. When I see pictures on the television or Internet, it seems like some far off place that I will never visit, so I push it out of my mind.

It isn't the movies. Just a few short miles from the coast of the United States, there are millions of people who live in conditions that most Americans find unfathomable. Unfortunately, Haiti is one of many poor nations throughout the world characterized by living conditions that limit people from having an adequate existence. Consider these global statistics:[7]

- More than 80 percent of humanity lives on less than ten dollars per day.
- According to UNICEF, twenty-four thousand children die *each day* due to poverty.
- About seventy-two million school age children in developing countries did not attend school in 2007.
- Nearly a billion people entered the twenty-first century unable to read a book or sign their name.
- 1.2 billion people in developing countries have inadequate access to water, and 2.6 billion go without access to basic sanitation.
- For the 1.9 billion children in the developing world:
  - Six hundred and forty million (one in three children) don't have adequate shelter
  - Two hundred and seventy million have no access to health services (one in seven children)
- In 2003, 10.6 million children died before they reached the age of five.
- 2.2 million children die each year because they are not immunized.

Unfortunately, poverty isn't limited to countries outside the United States. Consider these statistics right here in our own backyard:

- More than 49 million people, including 16.7 million children, live in households that experience hunger or the risk of hunger (one in seven U.S. households).[8]
- In 2008, more than 13 percent of US households lived below the poverty level.
- 1.5 million children are homeless each year.[9]
- Fifty percent of adults can't read on an eighth-grade level.[10]
- Twenty percent of Americans are functionally illiterate and read below a fifth-grade level.[11]
- Twenty percent of Americans read below the level necessary to earn a living wage.[12]

We have it good. And by "we", I am referring to me and just about everyone who has the wherewithal to purchase this book and spend their leisure time reading its contents. Most of us have more than we know what to do with in terms of possessions, which is far more than the majority of the people on Earth. If you have any doubt, ask yourself the following questions:

- When was the last time I questioned where I would get my next meal?
- Do I have access to dental care (toothpaste, toothbrush)?
- When was the last time I wondered where I would sleep?
- Do I have access to a daily hot shower?
- Was there ever any doubt in my life that I was going to have the opportunity to learn to read and graduate from high school?
- Do I have easy access to basic information?
- If I get sick, is there a doctor nearby that will be able to help me?
- Do I have access to the necessary prescriptions to keep my body healthy?
- Do I have choices in my diet so that I can choose healthy foods?
- Do I have regular access to clean drinking water?

As you can imagine, I could go on forever. If we were to carefully inspect every detail in our lives, we would find very few of us go without the basic necessities. We have access to everything we need to adequately sustain each of our fundamental needs. In addition, because of advancements in technology and infrastructure these items are available to us at a very reasonable cost. In other words, we live in an age of *abundance*, and for most of us, there is plenty to go around. Consequently, we don't lack or want for anything that is necessary to keep our stomachs full, a roof over our head, or address any medical needs that may arise.

WHY DON'T WE COUNT OUR BLESSINGS?

If we have it so good, then what's the problem? I believe that most of us forget how good we really have it. Instead of feeling blessed that we woke up in a warm bed, ate a fulfilling breakfast, and drove to work in a clean car, we focus the majority of our time and attention on the things we lack. We wake up each morning with a new set of complaints—from hating our jobs to having aches and pains—and spend the entire drive into the office stressing about issues with clients. Once we arrive, we hurriedly dive into our workload and focus on checking "to-dos" off a never-ending list. Eventually, the work day ends, and we return home feeling exhausted and numb. During the last few hours of the day prior to sleep, many people prefer sitting comatose in front of the television in order to de-stress from the day. The cycle never ends; even vacations are filled with thoughts about the looming chores and duties that await us at home.

Currently, I am dealing with a mild foot problem that has caused me pain for several months and has kept me from running, one of my favorite gym activities. When I wake up with pain in my foot, it's not uncommon for me to wonder why my life needs to be so difficult and why I'm not as healthy as other men my age.

Before you begin to feel sympathetic towards my situation, let me tell what I am still able to do with this foot challenge:

- Go to work (I have only missed about two days)
- Work out (I can still lift weights and ride the bike)
- Have fun with my kids (They don't need me to run around too much)
- Go out with friends (I just need to watch my beer intake)
- Sleep (I have only had a handful of restless nights)

I had this "I really have it great" revelation a few weeks ago at church when our pastor asked us to pray for one of our members. The woman, who is the same age as my wife and has two young children, is in the final stage of breast cancer and going into hospice. Moments after hearing this prayer request, I began to feel very guilty for complaining about my foot so much to my wife. I leaned over to Nicole and whispered, "The next time I complain about my foot, please remind me about our friend, Megan, and her family."

The million dollar question that many ask themselves is, "Why does it take an awful piece of news, like the death of a friend with small children, to help us gain perspective?" Why does it seem that we need a 2' x 4' hit across our foreheads before we look at our own lives and feel blessed for all that we have been given?

I believe that the reason we all suffer from this "perspective problem" is due to a society that consistently reinforces a "never good enough" mentality. Virtually every waking moment of our lives is filled with a message suggesting that no matter what we have achieved, we are not good enough and should be striving for more. We believe we should be focused on making more money, buying more stuff, and getting flatter abs. There is no stopping point. It's likely that many people reading this book will get to the end of their lives having out-earned and out-achieved many of their friends. However, they will probably look back and realize that they didn't enjoy any of it because no matter what was accomplished, it was never enough.

How did we get this way? I think that our current predicament, as with all of our predicaments, is directly related to our environments. We weren't born with the perspective problem, we learned it. This truth was illustrated when a close friend of mine told me about his daughter's recent mission trip to Nicaragua, where she helped build 15' x 15' cement block homes for families. His daughter was amazed at the conditions in which these people lived: they didn't have running water, restrooms or electricity. What most stunned her wasn't the poverty; it was how happy and content the Nicaraguans seemed to be with these conditions. They spent every day grateful for what they had been given, not what they were lacking.

If this behavior is learned, why did we choose to fill our heads with a way of thinking that keeps us from enjoying our lives? The answer is that we are being heavily influenced by billions of advertising dollars that insist our current life circumstances stink. Marketing 101 teaches that before someone will buy a product or service, he or she needs to feel pain in order to recognize that their life is incomplete without that product or service. Marketing guru Martin Lindstrom illustrates this point in his book, *Buyology*. Lindstrom conducted a three-year, seven million dollar study and concluded that the majority of advertising today is focused on the emotion of fear.[13]

*Fear exerts an extremely powerful effect on the brain. In fact, when fear-based advertising plays less on our generalized anxieties and more on our **insecurities about ourselves** (author's emphasis), it can be one of the most persuasive – and memorable – types of advertising out there. Given that, I predict we'll be seeing more and more* *marketing based on fear in the years to come. Remember, the more stress we're under in our world and the more fearful we are, the more we seek out solid foundations. The more we seek out solid foundations, the more we become dependent on dopamine. And the more dopamine surges through our brains, the more we want, well, stuff. It's as though we've climbed aboard a fast moving escalator and can't get off to save our lives.*

As you reflect on this extremely powerful (and a little disturbing) quote from Lindstrom, consider the following examples that help to emphasize his "fear" theory. Spend an hour in front of the television and you will undoubtedly see the following types of commercials. First, a young woman walks into the picture, almost in tears because she has a pimple the size of an apple on her forehead...and prom is just three days away! Thirty seconds later, after the application of some miracle cream, she has a "normal" complexion that compares with the rest of her ridiculously attractive, thin friends who are all piling into a Hummer limo for their ride to the big dance. What not so subtle message is the advertiser sending to their audience of teenage girls? *That's right, if you don't use our pimple cream, you will probably be unattractive and have to take your cousin to the prom.*

How about the Viagra and Cialis marketing campaigns? Their message to fifty-plus males is clear. If you want to please your mate you had better be able to perform, even if you are in the middle of mowing the lawn on a Saturday afternoon. Real men, they argue, have a responsibility to their wives and should be ashamed if they can't turn on the Casanova at the drop of a hat.

The next example is a personal favorite of mine—the hair restoration movement. On the left side of the screen, you see a pathetic bald sap that looks like he hasn't bathed in weeks; on the right side is the man after having hair plugs—smiling from ear to ear, relaxing on his fifty-foot yacht, and surrounded by women half his age in bikinis.

And finally, a discussion of this topic wouldn't be complete without considering the gym/exercise equipment/workout video advertising approach. At the beginning of each commercial we see a frumpily dressed, overweight individual holding a hot dog in one hand and a milkshake in the other. Seconds later, the same individual is in a bathing suit and has lost at least fifty pounds after just thirty days on the diet/workout routine. What really does it for me is the interview with the new "thin" version. The person usually says something like, "My life was so miserable just a few short months ago. I am so happy now that I can go to the pool with my kids."

My point isn't that we shouldn't live a healthier lifestyle, strive for a clear complexion, and improve our sex lives. The problem isn't that we spend too much time and energy trying to improve ourselves. Rather, the issue lies in being conditioned by the mass media to *always* feel inadequate. As soon as you get a clear complexion or have rock hard abs, there will be another advertising campaign insisting that your life won't mean a thing until you drive a Porsche. It never ends; no matter what you achieve, you always feel inadequate. The unfortunate consequence of this feeling of "never being good enough" is that it makes it extremely difficult to be grateful for what you have in your life.

THE IMPORTANCE OF BEING GRATEFUL

You may be saying to yourself, "So, I'm not grateful – who cares? It's my life and if I don't feel like giving thanks for my position in life, it's my choice." While I agree that it is your choice, I believe that being grateful is an absolutely critical component to living an extraordinary life. As I said earlier, gratitude keeps everything in perspective, and you can't live a fully satisfying and amazing life without perspective.

Your perspective is the lens through which you see the world, and this lens is more important than your circumstances. Think about that statement for just a minute: if you truly embrace this concept, *it will change your life.*[14] Once you believe that you have absolutely everything you need right this minute, you will view everything through a new lens—a lens that will help you to see the world the way it actually is, not the way the modern society portrays it to be.

Let's go back to the example concerning my friend's daughter who visited the Nicaraguan village. I neglected to mention that my friend's daughter told him she felt the Nicaraguan children were much happier and content with their lives than her friends and she. Keep in mind that the kids from Nicaragua don't have running water and sanitation, while our children rarely go more than 7.6 seconds without their every need being met. Such an example is that of my 7-year-old son, who needs a snack in between his snacks and believes that his heart will stop beating if he goes more than 5 minutes without constant entertainment.

Can you imagine what these poor Nicaraguan kids would do if I brought them to the United States for a visit? They would probably think that our modest home in the suburbs was a palace (surrounded by other very similarly sized palaces) and wonder why everyone was allowed to take a hot shower every day. In addition, try to visualize their shock if I announced that they were free to go to the kitchen and chose from a pantry or refrigerator full of food whenever they became hungry.

Another interesting example of perspective happened this past summer while I was visiting Denver, Colorado, for a speaking engagement. I grew up in Denver and wanted to visit some old friends, so I scheduled an extra day in the city. Before I checked into my hotel, I decided to swing by the old neighborhood. On my drive, I began to reminisce about the great memories I had concerning my street, my home, the park where I played soccer, and my old school.

As I turned onto my street, initially I thought I had the wrong block; the houses were a lot closer together than I remembered. In addition, they all seemed so tiny. But, there it was, 1913 South Leyden Street—I was in the right place. The neighbors probably thought I was nuts, but I parked, got out, and looked around. I clearly remember mowing this lawn and thinking that it took forever. My best friend Ricky's house was no more than a couple hundred feet from mine. Back in 1982, it seemed like a mile away. Pulling away from the curb, I called my mom and told her I could only remember that it was a big house with a big yard on a big street. It was hard for me to believe that my happy memories were from a neighborhood that I now hardly recognized. What happened?

I'll tell you what happened between 1982 and 2010: my perspective changed. In 1982, I was a twelve-year-old boy whose entire life revolved around a small neighborhood on the southeast side of Denver. At that time I had never been on an airplane and had very little travel experience other than our annual trip to my grandparents in Nebraska. Twenty-eight years later, I am a completely different person. I moved clear across the country, attended college, got married, had kids, and spent a week at Disney World less than one year after my wife and I visited Paris!

Your happiness and contentment with life is directly related to this lens called perspective. The clearer your lens, the more satisfied you will be; this satisfaction is a building block for living an extraordinary life. The link between happiness and gratitude became clear to me about five years ago when I read the results of a research project called, "Dimensions and Perspectives of Gratitude."[15] Here are a few of their findings[16] that I found to be fascinating.

- People who kept gratitude journals on a weekly basis "exercised more regularly, reported fewer physical symptoms, and felt better about their lives as a whole." These people were also more optimistic about their upcoming week.
- These same individuals were also more likely to make progress towards their important personal and professional goals.
- They had "more positive states of alertness, enthusiasm, determination, attentiveness and energy" than those who kept similar journals but didn't focus solely on what was going right in their lives.
- Here's the big one—"Grateful individuals place less importance on material goods; they are less likely to judge their own and others' success in terms of possessions accumulated; they are less envious of others; and are more likely to share their possessions with others relative to less grateful persons."

Keep in mind that the only change in the study participants' lives was the clarity of the lens through which they viewed life. They replaced the "What is going wrong in my life?" lens with a different one that helped them to see the positive aspects of their day. This simple change made a significant impact in virtually every aspect of their lives, including their relationships, their jobs, and their health.

Armed with this data, it's clear that no matter how much you earn, where you live, or the amount of toys you have in your garage, you won't be satisfied unless you change your perspective and replace your current lens with one that allows you to see that we live in a world of abundance filled with more than we could ever need.

PUTTING GRATITUDE INTO PRACTICE

Hopefully, by now you are convinced that living gratefully is a key component in your life. Unfortunately, convincing you of this fairly obvious concept is the easy part. Living a grateful lifestyle is probably one of the most difficult habits any human being can develop. I should know, I have been working at it for more than five years and still spend hours where I am consumed with scarcity thinking. It's tough. However, instead of going days or weeks focused on what I don't have, I am able to catch myself and get back on the right track fairly quickly. I think you will appreciate some of the simple strategies that have helped me along my journey.

Strategy #1 – The Gratitude List
Before you can make gratitude a daily ritual, you need to clarify exactly what it is for which you are thankful. When I ask most people this question, I get the standard answers of family, health, job, etc. There is nothing wrong with these answers, except for the fact that they are too vague and not specific enough. Vague answers elicit vague emotions, and if you remember from chapter one, one of the best ways to ensure that we make changes in our lives is to have powerful emotions associated with the change.

Consequently, the first step in developing the habit of being grateful is to begin with a detailed "gratitude list." While this list will be different for everyone, I think it should have the following categories and these types of entries. Your list should be much more specific than this. For example, in your health section, you may note that you were able to get a chronic illness under control with medicine.

HEALTH	Eyesight and hearing
FAMILY	Wonderful, loving and supportive parents
FRIENDS	Jeff S. — A great friend who empathizes with all of my professional challenges
PROFESSIONAL	A rewarding career that allows me to consistently develop new skills
MATERIAL	A beautiful home where I raise my family
EDUCATION	The opportunity and ability to graduate from high school and college
OTHER	The ability to go on fun vacations with friends and family

HEALTH	Ability to stand, walk and exercise
FAMILY	Wonderful, loving, and supportive in-laws
FRIENDS	Kevin O. — A great friend who help me through some personal issues
PROFESSIONAL	An outstanding group of clients that have become my friends and helped me to learn
MATERIAL	The furniture that fills our home
EDUCATION	The ability to read and absorb new information
OTHER	Our neighborhood and all of the great friends in the neighborhood

HEALTH	Lack of chronic illness
FAMILY	Close and meaningful relationships with both siblings
FRIENDS	Devin —A neighbor who makes me laugh, and with whom I have great conversations
PROFESSIONAL	A brand and an image in the marketplace that allow me to position myself as a respected leader
MATERIAL	Our clothes we wear
EDUCATION	Etc.
OTHER	My faith and spiritual journey

Before you move on, take a minute and think about why you are grateful.

HEALTH	
FAMILY	
FRIENDS	
PROFESSIONAL	
MATERIAL	
EDUCATION	
OTHER	

Strategy #2 – The Gratitude Journal

Putting together the gratitude list is a good start, but putting together this list and filing it in a drawer that is reviewed annually will not lead to a long-term change in your behavior. For this to become a habit (a behavior you practice regularly without thinking about it), you need to practice it on a regular basis and "regular" means at least three to five times a week.

It is impractical for you to rewrite a gratitude list three to five times a week; in addition, I know from experience that you will eventually get bored by reviewing the same gratitude list every day. As a result, I advise that you consider regular reflection in a gratitude journal. This reflection typically includes a brief summary of what went well (or is going well) in your daily life. It can be simple as "My sore back was feeling better today" all the way to "I was awarded a new project with our largest client." It doesn't matter.

The key to this behavior is that it shifts your focus from what went *wrong* today to what went *right* today. Once this slight shift in perspective becomes a habit, it can mean a huge change in your mindset. Consider your thought process when your spouse asks you how your day went. If you're like most, your brain is programmed to scan everything that happened and focus on the handful of items that got screwed up. You need to reprogram your brain to focus on the good, and daily reflection in a journal can help by forcing you to acknowledge the positive aspects of each and every day. You will be amazed on how differently your perspective becomes after you spend just a few minutes writing down what you accomplished during the previous twenty-four hours.

Strategy #3 – Stewardship

We have already laid the groundwork that most of us in developed countries have more than enough resources to live a satisfactory life, especially when compared to the rest of the world. In addition, we also discussed the concept that one of the main reasons we aren't grateful is because we are too focused on what we don't have, as opposed to what we do. Consequently, I believe that one of the most powerful strategies towards developing the habit of gratitude is to allocate a portion of our resources (time and money) towards those who are less fortunate.

As a developed nation (United States) we don't do a great job of giving to others. In April of 2010, the Organization for Economic Co-operation and Development calculated that the US ranks 19th in the world in giving as a percentage of gross national income.[17] Consider these statistics:

- In 2007, more than 34 percent of all wealth in the US was held by less than 1 percent of the population.[18]
- The wealthiest 1 percent own more than 45 percent of all stocks and mutual funds.[19]
- Less than 27 percent of Americans volunteer.[20]
- 23.4 percent of households earning less than one hundred thousand dollars per year give to charitable organizations. Their average contribution was three hundred and thirty dollars.[21]
- Only 48 percent of households with a yearly income of between one hundred and two hundred thousand dollars give to charitable organizations. Their average gift was just over five hundred and fifty dollars.[22]
- Only 62 percent of the wealthy (those earning between two hundred thousand and one million dollars per year) made charitable contributions.[23]
- Just over 60 percent of the very wealthy (those earning more than one million dollars annually) gave to charitable organizations.[24]

No matter how you slice and dice the data, the picture is clear. As a whole, Americans give a very small portion of their time and income to help those who are less fortunate. As I discussed earlier, I believe we have a scarcity mindset, and we believe that the key to our happiness is acquiring more than everyone else.

What does this have to do with developing a habit of gratitude? Making a meaningful contribution to others helps you to gain perspective, and as you now know, perspective is the lens through we see the world and make all of our judgments. Unless you get into the habit of actively learning about the needs of others and then making a significant contribution to help them out, you will continue to focus on yourself and all that you could acquire/accomplish. This mindset will keep you from developing the habit of gratitude.

Let's examine how this works. Imagine that you are driving home from work on Friday, and you are upset after receiving a five thousand dollar bonus for the quarter instead of the expected eight thousand dollars. As you walk into your 3,500 sq. ft. home, you are greeted by your spouse, who asks about your day. Twenty minutes later, after you feel that you have properly vented, you sit down with a beer in front of your fifty-one inch flat screen television to watch ESPN. Just as a commercial ends, your spouse enters the room and reminds you that you are taking the kids to the homeless shelter at 9 A.M. the next morning.

Saturday morning arrived rather quickly, and soon you found yourself and the kids piling out of the minivan and approaching the shelter. You are upset at your friend from church for tricking you to help out at the shelter; you have better things to do. After getting situated, you are introduced to a family of four who looks a little bit like your family; there is a mother, father, son, and daughter. The father has been unemployed for more than eighteen months, and they were forced to move into the shelter after their home was foreclosed. For a minute, you put yourself in his shoes and imagine what it would be like if you had absolutely no resources to pay for food and shelter for your family. Suddenly, the three thousand dollar bonus shortfall from the previous day seems unimportant, and you feel an overwhelming sense of gratitude for your current situation.

Unfortunately, as the statistics above indicate, nearly 75 percent of Americans have never been in this type of situation because they don't volunteer their time. The majority of those who volunteer recognize this feeling of gratitude. However, if you want giving back to others to help in your journey to develop the habit of gratitude, you need to make it a regular practice in your life. I suggest the following simple guidelines:

- Tithe your income to charitable organizations. That means that you should give 10 percent of your annual income to those who are in need.
- Schedule regular volunteer work into your calendar.

While these two simple strategies are very easy to comprehend, I know from past experience that most people will find them extremely difficult to put into practice. Don't get frustrated if you struggle. Remember, making any meaningful change in your life is going to be difficult. I promise that the rewards you will enjoy from developing the habit of gratitude will be enormous.

WHAT I REALLY WANT YOU TO REMEMBER...

1. We've Got It Good – If you're reading this book, you probably have more resources than more than 90 percent of the people on Earth. It's important to recognize that millions of people on this planet don't have enough to eat, clean drinking water, a warm bed to sleep in at night, or any hope of having a better life.

2. The Glass is Half Empty – Even though we have it good, we complain all the time about our current situation. The two main reasons are:

- The media (Internet, television, radio, print) has become hypercompetitive. As a result, the only way they can get our attention is to bombard us with bad news.
- The multi-billion dollar advertising industry focuses the majority of its efforts on convincing us that our lives are unsatisfactory and can only improve with their products.

3. Who Cares? – It's not just important to be grateful because the Bible says so; being grateful leads to a more satisfying life characterized by greater progress towards your goals, less stress, and improved relationships.

4. Making It Happen – Declaring that you are now going to be more grateful isn't enough. You need to make gratitude a part of your life using these simple strategies:

- Put together a gratitude list
- Start a gratitude journal
- Practice stewardship

CHAPTER 6
IMPROVE EVERY DAY

*"There is only one corner of
the universe you can be certain of
improving, and that's your own self."*

Aldous Huxley
Author – *Brave New World*

When engaged in the sales process with my prospects, it is always my goal to help them recognize and focus on areas where improvement is needed. Approximately 10 percent of these prospects will assure me there is no need to change or improve; they feel satisfied with their current situation. With all sincerity, I say, "Congratulations on your success," and then begin to tell them a little bit about one of the laws of thermodynamics, the law of entropy.

At a very basic level, this law states that *everything* in the universe is in a constant state of decay. In other words, you can't stay the same—you are either getting better or worse. It is that simple, and it applies to *everything* in your life. Think about how this law applies to you. If you don't work on your relationship with your spouse, what happens? How about your kids and your closest friends? What about your health? Isn't it important that you exercise regularly and consistently eat healthy foods? What happens if you take a break for six months?

Let's apply this lesson to the 10 percent of the business owners that tell me they don't want anything to change. What they don't realize is that they don't have a choice in the matter because, as the law of entropy tells us, unless you are getting better, you are getting worse. If their product/service's marketing is working today, chances are, it won't in the future. If the products/services have a solid hold in the market today, without constant improvement, they will lose this position in the future. It's a guarantee. Do you remember a company called MySpace®? In 2006, they averaged nineteen million visitors per day while Facebook® averaged five million.[25] At that point, MySpace seemed unbeatable. Guess what happened during the next two years? Facebook® out-innovated MySpace, and in January of 2008, they averaged 25.2 million visitors per day while MySpace was less than twenty-three million.[26]

If you are interested in living a truly extraordinary life, you must be committed to constant and never-ending improvement. There is no choice; the behavior that helped you get to your current location often won't get you to where you want to go. While I believe that this rule has applied since the beginning of time, it is much more critical in today's society than ever before. We are bombarded with more information than at any time in the history of the world. The ability to access information and instantly communicate that information to others has resulted in a society where constant change is expected and has become the norm. There is no going backwards; if you aren't improving, there is a good chance you will miss something.

The Japanese word for this dedication to constant improvement is called *Kaizen*, which is Japanese for "change for the better." After World War II, the Americans were interested in helping the Japanese rebuild their industries, and they brought in experts to assist. These experts helped the Japanese develop "a philosophy or practices that focus upon continuous improvement of processes in manufacturing, engineering, supporting business processes, and management."[27] This process was rolled out throughout many Japanese industries. It has helped them to achieve such great results that many Japanese companies, like Honda, Suzuki, and Toyota continue to use it today. In addition, this practice of constant improvement has been rolled out to corporations throughout the world and is standard practice at virtually every manufacturing plant on the planet.

If you're interested in living your extraordinary life, it's time to brush up on your Kaizen. Put another way, if you're ready for the journey towards an extraordinary life, you will need to commit yourself to constant and never-ending improvement. That means you need to be in the classroom every day, ready for another lesson, and I'll show you how throughout the remainder of this chapter.

SCHEDULE YOUR LEARNING

This commitment to constant and never-ending improvement will require you to make learning a regular part of your schedule. It is no different than going to work or the gym. If you don't prioritize this type of activity, it will never take place and will become like so many other discarded "resolutions" that you once deemed as important. In today's information society, there are countless opportunities to learn and improve. The key is to figure out which one works for you. After finding an opportunity that fits, make sure to create a system that's easy to follow and fits into your schedule.

However you decide to schedule learning into your daily life, there are some basic guidelines that you should follow. First, set a goal to read a certain number of non-fiction books each year. When I say read, I actually mean that you go to a book store, buy a book, hold it in your hands, and read it. The reason I recommend this approach is that there is value in holding a book in your hands, underlining passages that are important to you and writing notes at the end of a chapter. Once you do this, a book becomes more than just something you read; it is an important part of your learning journey. I recognize that with the advent of the Kindle®, the iPad®, and the Sony Reader®, this approach may make me sound like an old-timer, but I can't imagine that reading something on the computer is the same.

Shortly after you make the commitment to actually read a number of books during the next year, also consider purchasing audio books. This is important because it's likely that you spend a significant amount of time in your car during the workweek. Imagine if you were in the car for one hour a day and worked an average of two hundred and fifty days a year. At that rate you could listen to more than thirty books over the course of the year as long as you were able to give up sports radio and your favorite music station. While not as intellectually valuable as reading (it's impossible to concentrate 100 percent on the book while you are driving), listening to an audio book is a valuable use of drive time. In addition to non-fiction books concerning topics that are valuable to you, I also believe that it is important to keep up-to-date on current events because your ability to make informed decisions is influenced by the world around you, both personally and professionally. This is especially important as it relates politics. The United States is run by individuals who are selected by the people they represent. Unfortunately, most people don't take the time to learn about the issues and instead base their decisions on sound bytes. Elections have become popularity contests, won by the politicians who can raise the most money and look good in front of a camera. It's our responsibility to commit ourselves to constant education on the issues that affect our lives.

The best way to stay up-to-date on current events in society and in your business is to subscribe to a handful of monthly (most people don't have time for weekly) periodicals and a daily newspaper (I am okay if it's more convenient for you to read a daily newspaper online). As an executive coach and consultant to small and medium-sized business owners, I subscribe to *Inc®*, *Fast Company®*, and *Entrepreneur®*, which include relevant short articles that keep me abreast of the latest trends. As for the newspaper, I am a bit of a news junkie and read the local paper (*The Indianapolis Star*) and the *Wall Street Journal*.

Next, it's impossible to discuss learning methods without considering the information delivered over the Internet. With this medium, there are numerous options for collecting information, and by the time this book goes to print, many more will certainly have been added. To keep it manageable I will focus on the two methods that I consider to be the most valuable, blogs and podcasts.

As you may know, a blog is a "web log" or a website that is

usually maintained by one company or person and allows others to provide their opinion about the content of the site. What you may not know is how popular blogging has become. Blog search engine Technocrati (*www.technocrati.com*) estimates that one hundred seventy five thousand blogs are created each day and estimates that there are one hundred and thirteen million blogs, with about 7.5 million that are active. These active blogs are visited by more than one hundred and eighty four million bloggers, who post five hundred and seventy thousand posts every twenty four hours.[28]

While I don't recommend that you spend an enormous amount of time blogging, I do believe that you should pick a handful of those that you find valuable and read them on a regular basis. A blog allows you to digest bite-sized pieces of information that are typically very topical and relevant. Compare this to an old-fashioned book, which is dated weeks after it hits the stands. If you're not sure where to start, I recommend that you spend a few minutes on Technocrati, or Google your favorite author because, chances are, he or she has a blog. My favorite is Seth Godin's blog, which you can find at *http://sethgodin.typepad.com*.

Next, I would recommend that you consider listening to podcasts on a regular basis. A podcast is simply a media file (audio or video) that is updated on a regular basis. Like blogs, because setting up and maintaining a podcast is fairly simple, the number of active podcasts is significant and growing each day. The reason I recommend that you consider a regular audio podcast is that you can listen to it whenever you don't have the ability to read. For example, I listen to about four different sermons each week while I am at the gym. In addition, like blogs, podcasts are typically small chunks of relevant and topical information. To get started, I would recommend that you visit *www.podcast.com*.

Finally, to round out your learning, I encourage you to engage in some experiential education. By this, I typically mean workshops and seminars taught by professionals. These programs are different than the previous forms of learning because, typically, they force you to participate actively in the experience. This participation engages your brain in a way that is different from passive forms of learning, such as reading a book or listening to a podcast. Your ability to retain information improves greatly when you are actively engaged in the learning process.

The first step towards ensuring your constant improvement and learning is becoming a regular habit is to schedule some of this learning into your daily routine. This learning can take many different forms, and each day, technology makes it easier and more convenient. However, it needs to be scheduled and not just random.

SEE OPPORTUNITIES IN EVERY SITUATION

Many times, you are presented with opportunities to discover new information outside of your scheduled learning times. I teach a class for small business owners called Reach™, and the class takes place each week over a three-month period. At the beginning of each class I ask the room to answer the following question, "Write down an important lesson you have learned during the past seven days." The class soon learns "I'm not sure" isn't an acceptable answer, and here's why: every day is filled with countless opportunities to learn. Unfortunately, this is a foreign concept to most people because we are too busy checking off tasks on our "to-do" list, and we don't slow down and realize how much we learn in our daily lives.

For example, this past spring I spoke to a group of small business owners about how to build a business that operates without the owner being present. I have spoken on this topic hundreds of times and can deliver the speech in my sleep. As a result, you wouldn't expect me to view this speech as a learning opportunity. However, after the speech concluded, I took five minutes and jotted down the things I would do differently if I could turn back the clock and re-do the talk. I asked myself, "What did you learn from that environment, that stage, that lighting, that crowd, etc.?" This simple exercise has helped me to become a much better speaker over the years, and I imagine that I will continue to reflect after every speech until I decide to quit the profession. In other words, I will continue to practice Kaizen, or the commitment to constant and never-ending improvement.

Each of us has this same opportunity in our everyday lives, both personally and professionally. Let's look at a typical day: Imagine that you are having breakfast with an extremely important prospect at a restaurant near your office. You are starving and decide to order the Sunrise Special, which includes pancakes, eggs and enough bacon to choke a horse. By the time the meal is finished, you realize that you spent as much time eating as you did conversing with your guest. As you drive away, you should observe an important lesson: eat a small breakfast before the meeting so you can focus on what's important.

Shortly after you return to your office, you begin answering a handful of e-mails before you get to a long message from one of your coworkers. Seconds later, you get become furious at the tone and content of the message. You are so angry that you spend the next thirty minutes crafting the perfect response, followed by a satisfying click of the *send* button. Unfortunately, you have just begun a nearly two-hour long e-mail battle that keeps you from concentrating on anything else meaningful during this time frame. Finally, you decide that "enough is enough" and schedule a meeting with your coworker to discuss the issue. After a brief fifteen minute meeting, all is better. The lesson: never have an argument over e-mail.

Luckily, you get to have lunch by yourself and cool off for an hour. Refreshed, you head back to the office for a staff meeting that is scheduled to last from 1:30 – 3 P.M. About ten minutes into the meeting, you open your iPhone® and start checking your e-mail, justifying this behavior by reminding yourself that this meeting is always full of information that has absolutely nothing to do with your job. You often wonder why you attend these meetings in the first place. After the meeting's conclusion, you soon realize that you forgot to ask an important question during the meeting because you were preoccupied with your e-mail. You decide that you would rather find the answer to this question on your own than send an e-mail to the group and apologize for not paying attention during the meeting. Forty-five minutes later, you find the answer to the simple question that you should have addressed during the mandatory meeting. The lesson: put down the cell phone and pay attention during meetings.

As soon as you arrive home that evening you are greeted by your spouse, who indicates that he/she wants to have an important discussion with you about one of the neighborhood kids who isn't playing nice with your daughter. Tired and stressed out from the day, you wonder why it's necessary to have this unimportant conversation after a day full of important and *meaningful* challenges. Unfortunately, this thought influences your response to your spouse, and he/she becomes very upset with you. If you're paying attention, you will notice an extremely important lesson: you need to become an active listener and empathize with others, especially your spouse!

Finally, just as you are preparing your kids for bed, you notice an e-mail on your phone. Against your better judgment, you quickly check the message and realize that it is a client indicating that they are unhappy with your services. Instead of the fun and rewarding book reading and nightly tuck-in ritual with your kids, you rush through the entire process because you're obsessed with your response to the e-mail. How can you make certain that your kids don't suffer from your obsession with work? Turn off e-mail at night!

We are all blessed with multiple opportunities to learn, from the time we wake up in the morning until we close our eyes at night. There is no shortage. Regrettably, most people ignore these opportunities in their haste to check tasks off their to-do list. This leads to a day characterized with mistakes that could have easily been avoided had you simply taken the time to learn from the previous twenty-four hours. You sit in a classroom every day for at least sixteen hours in a class called *Life 101*, and you are both the professor and student. Take full advantage of each lesson, and you will be amazed at how much you learn and improve.

GET OUTSIDE YOUR COMFORT ZONE

At this point, we have discussed a handful of important strategies for educating yourself on a daily basis. If you take time each day to read a book, magazine, or blog, or listen to an audio book or podcast, you will undoubtedly learn and improve your skill sets, both personally and professionally. Additionally, if you make certain that you treat every situation throughout your day as an opportunity for self education, you are well on your way to becoming a master of Kaizen. Before we can complete this discussion about improvement, it's important that we address the most valuable and difficult method for bettering ourselves, getting outside of our comfort zones.

I regularly conduct a completely unscientific study on this topic. Each day I ask my clients, prospects, friends, and family what they have done recently to get outside of their comfort zone, and the unscientific results are telling. Human beings spend the majority of their days, consciously and subconsciously, doing whatever they can to stay in situations with which they are familiar and that cause the least amount of stress or anxiety. At some level we all want to feel satisfied and comfortable, and as a result, we avoid situations and circumstances that jeopardize our contentment.

Unfortunately, these situations, while uncomfortable, typically provide our *best* opportunity to learn and improve.

There are many reasons why we grow the most when we get outside our comfort zone. First, in a society dominated by constant activity, communication and busyness, our brains can get in an intellectual rut. In other words, technology has made it easy to accomplish a lot without stretching our cognitive capabilities. For example, you can teach class, attend a workshop, send one hundred e-mails, participate in a conference call, and complete the research necessary to write a book without leaving your office. Getting outside your comfort zone creates a pattern interrupt or an unexpected change that often leads to an alteration in behavior.

Assume for a minute that you are a financial analyst for a bank and your primary job responsibility is to crunch numbers in your cubical for eight hours a day, periodically preparing reports for upper management. Early one morning you receive an e-mail from your boss asking you to give a presentation to a group of clients visiting from all around the country. Although the information you will be presenting is no different than what you work on every single day, you have never been asked to speak in front of a group. This pattern interrupt changes the way you typically approach your workday and forces you to think differently by getting outside your comfort zone.

Another reason that getting outside your comfort zone is extremely valuable is that it is typically associated with a strong emotion. Events tied to these types of emotions have the best chance of impacting your behavior because they stand out from everything else that takes place in your life. In a day filled with information overload, it's likely that you will remember the incidents that caused you to feel anxiety, stress, or even great joy. In our previous example, it's likely that the financial analyst may have trouble sleeping the night before the presentation and may even have an upset stomach right before he addresses the group. This anxiety is (hopefully) followed by a great sense of accomplishment once it is completed. Chances are, he will never forget this incident, and even though he may never want to speak in front of a group again, the emotion associated with this experience will result in great growth and self-improvement.

I believe that each of you has an inner drive to accomplish big goals, with "big" being relevant to your unique situation. No matter the objective, it's unlikely that it can be achieved with your current set of skills or knowledge. You need to grow in order to achieve whatever it is that drives you and some of this growth must take place outside your comfort zone. Think back to your greatest accomplishments: Did you reach any of these without undertaking some task or exercise that was new and caused some anxiety? What about college? I am sure that you had more than one exam that kept you up at night. Weren't you nervous the morning of your first day at work? How about the day you got married? Didn't butterflies fill your stomach until the final "I do"? And finally, if you have kids, you *will never forget* that first day that you entered your home with an infant. All of these anxiety-filled moments represent significant accomplishments in your life that helped you to grow into the person you are today. You would be completely different had you not been forced outside of your comfort zone on each occasion.

My life is no different. My greatest accomplishments have been the result of a journey far outside of my comfort zone. One example stands out above the rest: I was thirty-two years old and my wife and I were contemplating having our first child. At the time, I was working at a software company and had realized that I was tired of working for other people. It was time for me to do something on my own, so I set out to buy my own company. My biggest challenge was that I had absolutely no idea where to start.

First, I just started talking about buying a business. I had convinced myself that if enough people heard me mention my interest in purchasing a new business, someone would call me out of the blue with a great opportunity. Months later, I decided that I needed a new tactic and visited Barnes & Noble® to purchase a couple of books on the topic of identifying a good company to purchase (unfortunately, "Buying a Business for Dummies" didn't exist). These books provided me with a foundational understanding of the basics and helped me to realize that I needed some assistance in my search. As a result, I decided to engage the services of a business broker.

Business brokers are interested in helping business owners sell their extremely hard-to-value companies at the highest price possible; and they don't get paid unless the business sells. As a result, typically, they are only interested in working with buyers who have a significant amount of cash and/or experience in purchasing a business. A thirty-something-year-old with very little cash who has gotten bored with corporate America (me) isn't the greatest prospect. Despite this fact, I was able to get a few brokers to spend some time with me, and they allowed me to look at some deals. While I learned a great deal, this eight-hour weekly extracurricular exercise led nowhere, and after looking for nearly a year, I was beginning to get a bit frustrated.

Then, one Sunday afternoon while I was reviewing the "Business Opportunities" classified section in the newspaper, something caught my eye. It was an invitation to the **FranNet**™ - *Free Franchise Seminar*, a ninety-minute workshop that promised to provide all I needed to know about buying the right franchise. Minutes after seeing the ad, I called the number and signed up, even though I had never considered buying a franchise before. Later that week, I sat in a hotel conference room with a dozen or so other burned-out corporate guys, hoping to hear some magic. While I didn't exactly hear magic, I was intrigued enough to meet with the presenter and later signed an agreement to begin another eight hour a week extracurricular search for a business to buy.

Less than two weeks after I signed the agreement, I was on the phone with the national sales director of a residential cleaning service who was trying to convince me that cleaning homes was the key to riches. After that, I talked to a carpet cleaning franchise and a few others that seemed interesting. Each time, when I was about ready to push through to the next step and agree to visit the franchisor, I got cold feet and backed out. Looking back, I now realize that although it was a bunch of effort, spending eight hours per week reviewing financials, meeting with brokers, and calling franchisors was within my comfort zone. However, actually spending money to visit a franchisor or "take the next step" was, for some reason, outside my comfort zone; as a result, I never pulled the trigger.

Something had to change or I was forever going to be the guy looking to buy a business; that something was a franchise advisor named Meri Cronk. After about sixty days of looking at several businesses with no real progress, Meri asked if we could meet one day over my lunch break. Meri was an extremely nice and thoughtful person who was very gently nudging me in the direction of buying a franchise. However, in this meeting, I got a slightly different Meri. Shortly after I sat down, she went through a brief rundown of all of the businesses that I had looked at and my reasons for passing on each one. Then, she looked me right in the eye and said, "CJ, you don't really want to buy a business. You are just bored with your career. I think that continuing to look is a waste of both your and my time."

Initially, I was furious. How dare she tell me that I was not ready to buy a business! It wasn't my fault that she couldn't find a fit that made sense for my situation. A few days later, I was sitting on the back porch one warm spring evening and I realized something that would change my life forever. She was right. I was just bored and was wasting everyone's time. The time had come for me to decide if I was ready to take a risk and do something completely different with my life. I had to decide if I was ready to get outside of my comfort zone, because if I didn't, nothing would change.

Six weeks later, I wrote a check for fifteen thousand dollars (partial payment) to *Action International* to buy a business-coaching franchise. Bear in mind that six weeks earlier, I had never even heard of business coaching. The next thing you know, I quit my job, took the majority of our savings and started a new business from scratch. In addition, this entire life transformation took place five days before we had our first child. I was so far outside of my comfort zone that the whole thing seemed surreal.

The first year was tough. I was making fifty to one hundred cold calls a day from my basement and working seventy-plus hours a week. It's also important to note that during the first few months of my business I was also getting a crash course on how to be a dad. While I would not recommend this approach to anyone, I can tell you that I learned more about myself and my capabilities in that first twelve months than I had learned in the first ten years of my career.

The most valuable lessons in life occur outside your comfort zone. If you have any doubt, quit your job a month before you have a child and start a business from scratch.

ONE DAY AT A TIME

I'll assume that while you've found this discussion about the importance of learning to be valuable, it's unlikely that you have read anything new in the past fifteen pages. But, don't forget what Dr. Covey taught us, "To know and not to do, is really not to know." We know that it's important to learn and improve every day, but for a variety of reasons (no time, it's too hard, it never works, etc.) we don't work at it. Another reason that most people tend to overlook: the average person struggles to make constant improvement a regular habit because every time they face a challenge, they want to know the perfect answer *immediately* instead of focusing on smaller, incremental progress.

Here's a typical story I hear from a client. Sometime during one of our first few meetings of 2010, I sat down with my client and reviewed the 2009 results. Unfortunately, his company lost seventy-five thousand dollars and saw sales decline by 15 percent. He was extremely frustrated and wondered if he should shut down the company. His depression only grew worse after a conversation with a colleague, who indicated that his business had had a good year and he looked forward to 2010 being even better. The discouraged owner confided in me, "I am not even close to having the type of company I thought I would have at this point in my career," and wondered aloud, "Where did I go wrong?"

Next, he asked, "How do I grow my sales back to 2008 levels and get back to the position where I am able to save a couple hundred thousand a year?" I responded with a terse, "You don't." By that, I meant that I didn't advise my client to focus on getting his current sales back to 2008 levels. The numbers from

☐ YOUR COMFORT ZONE
■ WHERE THE MAGIC HAPPENS

2008 represented a 54 percent increase from where he was at the moment. If he chose to focus on the number he would only get frustrated, because no matter how hard he worked or what decisions he made, he would still be far away from his goal.

As this example illustrates, most people want all the answers immediately and they don't value learning in small increments. In fact, most find it extremely frustrating. Unfortunately, focusing on incremental progress is the best way to approach learning. Here's the advice that I would give my client who is interested in an immediate return to his or her 2008 profits: slow down and focus on the fundamentals. I would ask the following questions in this exact order because it doesn't make sense to grow revenue if we don't understand how much we are making on each sale. As a result, we would not move from one question until the current one had been answered.

1. What are our gross margins on each product/service? Have they changed? Why?
2. What is our fixed overhead as a percentage of sales? Is it too high? Is it the right time to correct?
3. Have our target market(s) changed? If yes, how?
4. Are our current products/services still valuable in each of these markets? If not, why not?
5. Which of our products is the most profitable?
6. How many leads are we generating in each market? Where are these leads coming from?
7. What is our conversion rate? Is it getting better or worse? Why?

As we move down the list, I would provide tactical solutions (a.k.a., answers) as appropriate. For example, if I wasn't satisfied that the owner understood his or her target market, I would recommend an exercise to gain clarity before I suggested any new lead-generating strategies. This process will be extremely frustrating for the owner because he or she wants the problem solved immediately. As a result, this approach, which requires small incremental lessons, causes many people to quit because they believe that the goal is unachievable. In reality, they don't have the patience to focus on the small tactical objectives along the path to the bigger goal.

If you want to avoid this frustration, remember that constant and never-ending improvement is a journey that is typically measured with small meaningful lessons. To use a baseball metaphor, instead of always trying to smash a home run, you should instead worry about hitting singles if your team's expectation is a winning record. In other words, focus your learning into daily bite-sized increments and don't expect an instant answer to your most difficult challenges. This will make even the most difficult challenges seem manageable and will always lead to better results in the end.

WHAT I REALLY WANT YOU TO REMEMBER...

1. You're Falling Apart – Well, not really. However, it is true that everything in the universe is in a constant and gradual state of decay. As a result, you are either getting better or you're getting worse; there is no maintaining the status quo.

2. The Habit of Learning – If you are truly committed to developing a habit of constant self-improvement, then you need to schedule learning opportunities into your daily life. These include:

- Reading
- Audio books
- Blogs
- Podcasts
- Workshops and seminars

3. Opportunities are Everywhere – Even though you may not have time to read a book or listen to a podcast, there are countless opportunities to learn in your everyday life. You just need to pay closer attention and take some time to reflect.

4. Uncomfortable is OK – The most valuable lessons in your life will occur outside of your comfort zone. You need to embrace situations that make you uncomfortable on a regular basis.

5. Carpe Diem – Don't expect all of the answers to come at you instantly. The best way to achieve long-term growth is to focus on daily, incremental lessons.

CHAPTER 7
LIVE IN THE MOMENT

*"I try to learn from the past, but
I plan for the future by focusing
exclusively on the present.
That's where the fun is."*

Donald Trump
Entrepreneur

The present moment is all that we have. That is it. The only way that you can truly get the most out of the words on this page is to forget about the past, disregard the future, and live exclusively in this present moment—it is all that really matters. The minute you truly embrace and live this truth, your life will be changed forever. More than two thousand years ago Jesus advised us: "Don't worry about tomorrow, for tomorrow will bring its own worries. Today's trouble is enough for today."[29] Since then, many philosophers, teachers, and authors have spoken about this truth, and many spiritual movements consider this truth to be their foundation. While I may not be ready to take up a new religion, I do agree that living an extraordinary life must be built upon a foundation of living in the moment.

I began to understand the power and importance of living in the moment in 2004 when I was attending a conference in Las Vegas with my fellow franchisees. The speaker provided us with a statistic, indicating that the average busy professional allocates his or her time in the following manner:

- *Past Events – 30 percent*
- *Present Event – 15 percent*
- *Future Events – 55 percent*

These statistics suggested that just about everyone in that conference room spent the majority of their waking hours focused on what they had done in the past or what they were going to do in the future instead of what was taking place in the present. After reflecting on these statistics, I was a little ashamed to admit that my thought patterns were extremely similar to everyone else. Next, this speaker advocated that the most successful, content, and satisfied professionals shared a very different breakdown in how they spent their time, arguing that time should be allocated in the following fashion:

- *Past Events (5%)* – Occasionally, we should take a moment to reflect on the past and ensure that we learn and don't make the same mistakes twice.
- *Present Event (85%)* – The majority of our waking hours should be spent in the present moment.
- *Future Events (15%)* – It makes sense to spend a small portion of our time planning for future activities.

It made sense. Why would you constantly sacrifice the current moment, just to make certain that you are more prepared for a future moment or that you have carefully analyzed a past event? What value does all of this preparation and analysis provide if you can never enjoy what you are currently doing?

WHAT'S SO GREAT ABOUT THE PRESENT?

The present moment is all that we have, and the absolute best book on this topic is the *The Power of Now* by Eckhart Tolle. I consider it to be one of the most insightful and helpful books I have ever read because it helped me understand the notion that the present moment (or the Now) is all that matters. One of the many concepts that really struck me was Tolle's discussion about what he calls the "delusion of time".

To be identified with your mind is to be trapped in time: the compulsion to live almost exclusively through memory and anticipation. This creates an endless preoccupation with past and future and an unwillingness to honor and acknowledge the present moment and allow it to be. The compulsion arises because the past gives you an identity and the future holds the promise of salvation, of fulfillment in whatever form. Both are illusions.

Time isn't precious at all, because it is an illusion.

What you perceive as precious is not time but the one point that is out of time: the Now. That is precious indeed. The more you are focused on time – past and future – the more you miss the Now, the most precious thing there is.[30]

Unless you are getting your Masters in Philosophy, you may have to re-read this quote a few times for it to make sense and sink in completely. I know I did. But once you grasp his message, I think you will find it to be both profound and enlightening; you will also begin to understand why living in the present is an essential ingredient to living your extraordinary life.

After reading this passage three or four times, I finally began to take hold of the concept that if I identify completely with my mind, I will be "trapped in time." Here's my interpretation of this concept: Our tendency as busy adults in 2010 is to live in a state of constant over-analysis, always grading our performance against a set of societal norms. No matter how we measure up, the analysis never ends and we never fully appreciate the moment. While I believe that some analysis is helpful (e.g., *What did I learn from this past situation?* or *How should I best plan for tomorrow?*), I do agree with Tolle that we need to be careful and not become trapped by this non-stop examination.

Tolle points out that our tendency to overanalyze results in "the compulsion to live almost exclusively through memory and anticipation."[31] Basically, he states that instead of living in the Now, we are programmed to focus on what we did or didn't accomplish in the past or what will happen in the future. He points out, "The compulsion arises because the past gives you an identity and the future holds the promise of salvation, of fulfillment in whatever form."[32] In other words, we become trapped by our minds because we measure our self-worth (identity) by what we have accomplished. Furthermore, we believe that our success, satisfaction, and contentment lie in the future instead of the present moment.

At this point, I can imagine a rational person reasoning that this "compulsion" Tolle refers to is a natural and helpful component in achieving more personal and professional success in life. You might believe that if you don't multitask and engage your mind in multiple thought patterns at a time, you aren't being as productive as you could. I would agree that the constant focus on past and present may help you to accomplish more personally and professionally. However, I am certain that while this practice may help you put more money in your bank account, it will not help you lead an extraordinary life because it will be a life filled with accumulation, not experience. Do you really want to out-achieve everyone and not truly enjoy any of it because you chose not to savor the moment?

Imagine the following situation: You are on vacation with your family at the beach, and your two-year-old son is about to enter the ocean for the first time. As he approaches the water, a look of curiosity mixed with fear comes across his face. He shrieks when his first few steps result in water splashing up into his face, and he runs back up into your arms. After a little negotiating, you convince the boy to give it another try. This time, he enters sideways and quickly gains confidence as the warm water laps up against his tiny legs. Then, it happens; he turns his head and looks up at you with a smile from ear-to-ear, laughing hysterically. Your heart swells with pride and joy as you realize you never want to forget this moment as long as you live. It is highly unlikely that you would allow anything at all to interrupt this milestone with your son because, at some level, you realize that nothing, no past accomplishment nor future pleasure, is more important than this moment.

Now, consider a circumstance in your professional life, a Monday morning staff meeting. Minutes after your boss calls the meeting to order, your mind begins to drift and you think about all of the work that needs to be accomplished after this routine gathering is completed. You convince yourself that this is one of those frequent circumstances where it makes sense to focus on the future rather than live in the Now. There are so many e-mails that require your attention and so many voicemails to return. It almost seems negligent to pay attention to the content of this meeting instead of worrying about what you are going to do next.

Let's assume that I agree with your rationale. If that is the case, here is the only thing that makes sense and is fair to everyone in attendance: Get up and leave the meeting. If you aren't giving this meeting your full attention, it is a complete waste of your time. If that suggestion seems a bit drastic, what if you considered actually paying attention and living in the moment? You might be surprised at just a few of the benefits that you would get from this approach including:

- Earning the respect of the other members at the meeting.
- Developing a better relationship with your boss and the others attending this meeting.
- Avoiding the eleven e-mails you need to send to follow up on details you would have gotten had you paid attention.
- Learning more about the company, including your current challenges and opportunities.
- Identifying opportunities to play a larger role in the organization.

In both of these examples, living in the Now greatly increases the value you receive out of the event. Personally, you will never forget the magical smile of your son as he steps into the ocean for the first time. Professionally, being the one person who actually pays attention during a routine staff meeting can impress your boss, give you insight into an important project, and make you more productive.

Before I move on, let me say a little more about the link between living in the present and professional productivity, because the idea that eliminating distractions can make you more productive flies in the face of just about everything you hear in the media. As we discussed in chapter 3, can you imagine a marketing campaign for a cell phone that only allows you to send and receive calls? In 2010, we are told that the more distractions, the better. This is a big lie designed to sell electronic devices (of which I own many).

The truth is that constant distractions can kill your productivity. In fact, research from Professor Piers Steel of Calgary University suggests that the beeps notifying the arrival of e-mail cause a domestic drop of .5 percent in the domestic GDP in the US, equating to more than seventy billion dollars per year.[33] Picture yourself sitting at your desk working on an important document that requires a high level of concentration. Out of the corner of your eye, you notice a little yellow envelope has suddenly appeared in the lower right hand corner of your computer screen. Despite the fact that you receive more than one hundred envelopes per day, you can't resist the urge to click open your e-mail and check the message. Seconds later, you delete another e-newsletter from someone you can't remember meeting and return to your document. Even though you were only distracted for a few seconds, don't you think it will take a while for you to regain your concentration? Can you imagine how much this would delay the completion of your project if you took a dozen e-mail breaks over an hour?

No matter how much we convince ourselves otherwise, if we are working on something that requires any amount of intellectual concentration, we can't effectively multitask because something will suffer. You can't have a phone conversation with a client while at the same time responding to an e-mail and expect to do either one effectively. A study published in the August 2009 issue of *The*

Proceedings of the National Academy of Sciences suggested that individuals who multitasked more frequently than others were less effective at basic comprehension tests than their peers who "spent less time simultaneously reading e-mail, surfing the web, talking on the phone and watching TV."[34]

The bottom line is this: Unless you are a surgeon, your wife is going to have a baby any day now, your office is on fire, or you work the McDonald's drive-thru, I can think of very few instances where it makes sense to allow distractions to interrupt the present moment. Let me say it again, *the present moment is all we have.* The past is just a fading memory, and the future is an event that will eventually take care of itself.

WHY IS IT SO DIFFICULT?

Before you jot down "live in the moment" on your to-do list, let me warn you that it is an extremely difficult task, and I don't know anyone who has completely mastered this habit. In fact, as soon as I can convince Mr. Tolle to have lunch with me, I plan on letting him know that I think it's virtually impossible for the average human being to focus exclusively on the Now. I didn't say it can't be done, nor that we shouldn't always endeavor to live in the present, I just said that it's much easier said than done. Unfortunately, as I complete this thought, I am reminded of what Dr. Covey taught us, "To know and not to do is really not to know."

Before I discuss what makes living in the present so challenging, let's take a minute to reflect on the past. Imagine for a minute that I had a time machine and was able to transport you back to 1970, just forty years ago. In addition to the fact that your jeans flared at the bottom, your hair was longer (unless you are challenged in the hair department, like myself) and your shirt collars were twelve inches long, life was very, very different.

An average day at the office would look nothing like it does in 2010. The main differences lie in the way in which we receive and process information. In 1970, a person would arrive at the office and either attend a meeting, review a report, or make a phone call. In 2010, it's unlikely that one gets more than a few minutes into the day without checking an e-mail. In 1970, an entire day may consist of a handful of conversations with a few customers, prospects, and employees. In 2010, one will have the same amount of communication with others by the time he or she gets a second cup of coffee.

Let's compare the typical hour-long meeting at the office in 1970 to a similar meeting we would have today. In 1970, one had virtually no distractions, except a secretary entering the office to offer more refreshments. In 2010, I would be surprised if a person could go more than two minutes without checking his or her mobile phone for a text, e-mail, or other update. An unintended result of this instant access to communication/information is that people no longer pay attention in meetings because they know there will be an e-mail follow-up; if they missed something, they can send a mass message to all attendees in seconds and request a follow-up. In 1970, you had to listen carefully to every topic; if you missed something, you were in trouble because this meeting represented the only way this information was being disseminated to the group.

In 1970, as soon as the day ended and you got into the car, you had an opportunity to mentally unwind from work because all you could do was listen to the radio on the drive home. In 2010, the drive home is merely an extension of the work day, filled with phone calls, texts, and e-mail messages (regardless of the danger involved with driving and responding to an electronic message).

The differences continue once you pull into your driveway. In 1970, you would enter the house and have a few simple options; talk to your spouse, play with the kids, read the paper (to learn about current events from the previous day), or watch one of three channels on the television. In 2010, we have an unlimited choice of how to be entertained. You could turn on the television and watch one of hundreds of channels on virtually any topic you could imagine, or you may choose to watch a television show that you previously recorded with your DVR/TiVo®. If five hundred channels don't seem like enough options, you may choose to surf the Internet to check on your fantasy football team, the weather for the weekend, or the dating status of the American Idol® contestants. Many busy professionals choose to continue working by checking e-mail on their cell phone. Unfortunately, a conversation with the spouse or kids seems so 1970's.

In 1970, we were constantly striving to improve and get better. As a result, we constantly had our eye on the future and what we were hoping to accomplish. However, because we could only do so many things at once, it was easier to live in the present. The average American is *suffering* from an information overload. And yes, I did say suffering, because while I believe that there are some extremely positive aspects to all of this information, I feel that it can (and often does) hurt the quality of our lives, both personally and professionally. All of these distractions have helped to create a culture filled with busy people who expect multiple channels of visual or auditory stimuli, from the moment they open their eyes until they drift off to sleep (usually with the television on in the background). As we discussed in chapter 3, the average American has become addicted to urgency, and this addiction makes it extremely difficult to focus on one thing at a time.

Not only do we find it difficult to focus on one thing (or live in the present moment), we have convinced ourselves that doing so is a sign of laziness. We aim for maximum productivity and believe that the only way to achieve this productivity is to engage our brain with multiple activities at once. As I stated earlier, it has become part of our culture; as independent as we would like to think we are, each of us is highly influenced by the environment in which we live.

How does today's environment shape our lives and contribute to our addiction to nonstop busyness and instant gratification? Instead of providing you with a list of the many examples that exist, I will tell you about a story that takes place on warm summer evenings in my neighborhood.

Every Friday night, three to five couples all gather on the back porch of one of our neighbors (Steve and Barb) to drink a few beers, eat some dinner (usually takeout pizza), and enjoy each other's company. My wife and I look forward to this evening all week long because our kids all love to play together, it's a great group of people who have become some of our closest friends, and we're always laughing. Nicole and I usually arrive first, claim our spots on the porch with Steve and Barb, and engage in some light "How was your week?" conversations. Over the next hour the other couples wander in, with the Sanders (Devin and Amy) arriving last.

The night is characterized by a lot of laughter, stories about our kids, and the inevitable Nicole and CJ countdown—we typically leave first. At first glance, this would seem no different than a warm summer evening in 1972. Let's look a little deeper. One of the parents begins to tell us about their daughter's softball schedule for the summer. Before I tell you some of the details that I can remember, please note that she is thirteen years old. They are beginning to enter the "tournament" season that includes travelling each Friday through Sunday. During the week, some of the girls on the team spend time with their hitting and/ or pitching coaches. That is not a misprint, I said "hitting and/or pitching" coaches for thirteen-year-old girls softball. As their story concludes, I begin to reminisce on my own summer schedule as a thirteen-year-old in Denver—wake up, eat breakfast, go to the pool, shower, go to bed, repeat. Our kids are convinced that they need to be in some sort of organized activity every minute of the day *because all of the other kids are doing it.* By the way, as I write this sentence, I am reminded that I wanted to look into a summer basketball camp for my seven-year-old son.

Next, Amy gets a call from her husband, Devin, who is out of town for work. She hangs up the phone and informs the group that he always forgets something at home when he travels; this time it was underwear, a belt, and shoes. Seconds later, I text Devin and tell him that his wife is talking about what kind of underwear he buys, hoping to engage him in a long text conversation about underwear while I was sitting on the back porch with good friends laughing and having fun. Looking up from the table, I notice that Amy and Barb are sending texts and Jeff is checking his e-mail.

The conversation meanders from one funny topic to another, and we stumble across movie quotes. I ask the group if they have ever heard the spoof on *A Few Good Men* about selling and lap dances. No one had any idea what I was talking about. In 1972, we would have moved on to another topic. However, by the time we were ready to switch subjects, Jeff had pulled up the exact spoof I was referencing on YouTube® and all of the guys gathered around his Blackberry® to watch while the ladies begin discussing *Sex in the City 2.*

Please note that there is absolutely nothing inherently *wrong* with this evening. We all enjoy spending time with each other, telling stories, drinking beer, and laughing hysterically. The point of this simple example is to illustrate that at no time of the day do we feel it's okay to focus solely on one task or event. Our brains have become conditioned to anticipate multiple interruptions in everything that we do, no matter how significant or important our current activity may be. If you have any doubt, spend a few minutes "people watching" at your next wedding and see how many people check their phones during the ceremony.

CAN WE CHANGE?

The 1970s are gone, and unless you are interested in moving to a remote island without Wi-Fi or a cell tower, you can't go back to the days where your kids could just play all summer long and you could have a conversation with your spouse or neighbors without constant interruptions. Good or bad, the lazy days of the 1970s aren't coming back. Our future is going to be filled with technological advances designed to provide you with more information that is quicker, easier and less expensive. In fact, I half expect there to be a tool that will read my mind and display instant Google results to my latest thoughts right above my bald head.

If that's the case, what can we do to develop the habit of living in the moment or the Now? I believe that there are a handful of simple and fundamental changes that we can make in our lives that will help us to concentrate on one task at a time; I will separate these into personal and professional. However, you will note that with instant access to information, it is increasingly difficult to separate the two categories.

Professional

Shut Your Door – Most professionals have convinced themselves that they want to have an Open Door Policy in their workplaces where you can walk into anyone's office at anytime and interrupt his or her efforts. This is ridiculous, and I get in arguments with leaders on a weekly basis about changing this practice in their office. Concentration is an absolute critical component to productivity. Every time you allow someone to enter your office unannounced you allow them to break your concentration, and this *always* leads to a reduction in productivity. In addition, the Open Door Policy leads to a corporate culture where people become lazy instead of figuring out solutions on their own; the instant they have a question, they leap up from their desks and go bug someone else looking for instant gratification. If you don't have an office, consider putting headphones in/on your ears and set the expectation that when they are on, you are not to be interrupted.

Turn off Your E-mail – Here's a technology tip for those of you who spend the majority of your day staring at a computer screen. You can click the red "x" in the upper right hand corner of MS Outlook and your computer will not explode—I promise. Checking e-mail while working on other projects breaks your concentration, even if all you do is delete an unwanted message. Try checking your e-mail once every few hours. Trust me, the captain of your fantasy football team can wait two hours to hear if you can make it to the draft party.

Get Rid of Your Smart Phone – I intentionally waited until the book was past the halfway point to provide this advice because for most people, it is like asking my wife to give up chocolate—*non-negotiable*. Having an electronic device that has the capability to connect with anyone instantly and access any information you could ever imagine *virtually eliminates* your ability to live in the present. It's impossible to give your full attention to what you are currently doing if you hear that little beep that indicates a new e-mail, text message, or call has arrived. For those of you who feel that setting your phone to vibrate is the answer: you are just kidding yourself. If this advice seems ridiculous (which I am sure it does), at least meet me halfway and turn off your phone whenever you are having a conversation with someone else.

Personal

Leave Your Laptop at the Office – If you bring your laptop home, plug it into an outlet, and keep it in home office, your brain thinks you are still at work. Here's why: every time you walk by that home office, you will be tempted to walk in and jiggle the mouse to see if anyone has sent you an e-mail. If you work out of your home, then turn your computer off when you have decided that the workday is over.

Turn Your Phone Off as Soon as the Workday Ends –Yes, I did say "off", not set to vibrate. I am always amazed when I am at my son's baseball game and half of the parents are checking e-mail or talking on their cell phones. Similar to your laptop, if your phone is on and you can receive messages relating to work, your brain thinks that you are always at work. Now, because I am committed to full disclosure, I must admit that I used to bring the *Wall Street Journal* to the games until my wife sarcastically pointed out that "Mr. Live in the Moment" couldn't go six innings without any outside distractions.

Turn the Television Off – I read somewhere that most people leave the television on all day, even if they aren't watching it. Here's the obvious problem with that practice. The sights and sounds coming from your television (which if you live in my neighborhood is at least forty-two inches in diameter) are distracting and keep you from concentrating on any one thing. The same goes for eating out; my wife knows that if we go to a restaurant with sports on in the background, I might as well not even be there. I would like to say that I am ready to change this piece of advice to "Get Rid of Your Television", but I am not quite there (although I hope to be someday). *Baby steps*, I tell myself.

There you have it, six simple strategies for living in the present. Chances are high that I am not the first person to provide you with this advice. We know that these distractions are negatively affecting our quality of life, but like slowing down to view an accident along the side of the road, we can't seem to stop. I can empathize; living in the moment is like learning to write with your opposite hand or trying to quit smoking: it's hard. But I promise the rewards are well worth the effort. Our creator gave us five senses to *enjoy* life. We aren't on this earth to simply out-accomplish everyone else. An extraordinary life is about living in the moment and not the longest obituary.

WHAT I REALLY WANT YOU TO REMEMBER...

1. **The Present is All We Have** – Most people live in the past or the future. When you really think about it, all we ever have is the present moment: this is where we enjoy all of the joy and satisfaction in our lives.

2. **You Can't Do It All** – Studies are now showing that the average human being can't multitask on activities that require intellectual concentration. If you do two things at once (talk on the phone while sending an e-mail), the quality of one of these tasks will suffer.

3. **It's Hard** – The advances in information technology have made it really, really hard to live exclusively in the moment. Our environment has conditioned us to expect and even look forward to constant interruptions in whatever we are doing.

4. **You Can Change** – Although it's hard, there are some simple fundamental habits you can develop that will help you to live in the present, both professionally and personally.
   - Professionally
     - Shut your door
     - Turn off your e-mail
     - Get rid of your smart phone
   - Personally
     - Leave your laptop at the office
     - Turn off your cell phone
     - Turn off your television

CHAPTER 8
CHOOSE YOUR FUTURE

"It is our choices that show what we truly are, far more than our abilities."

JK Rowling
Creator of Harry Potter

It was 10 A.M. on a Tuesday morning, and I had just finished teaching a class to a group of business owners. My assistant, Erin, reminded me that I had a 10:30 A.M. speaking engagement for a new client who had brought in their national sales force to hear my message. She placed the MapQuest™ directions next to my bag and alerted me that the trip looked like it would take about fifteen minutes. I assumed that the MapQuest™ estimate was counting on my driving at the normal speed limit, and I decided to quickly check e-mail. At approximately 10:15 A.M. I closed my laptop, grabbed the directions, and headed out the door without a care in the world.

Unfortunately, the MapQuest™ route was a little vague, and I got a little lost. At 10:36 A.M. my phone rang with a call from Jamar, my VP of Sales. He had just received a call from our brand-new client (who had people in from all over the country) wondering when I planned on arriving. I apologized and told him that I would be there in five minutes. Immediately after I hung up the phone, the following thought popped into my head, "How in the world could Erin allow me to sit at my office until 10:15 A.M.? She and I are going to have a very uncomfortable conversation when I get back to the office. How did she think I was going to make it to this appointment on time?"

Let's review the facts. I was finished with my class at 10 A.M., at which point Erin reminded me that I had an appointment at a new client's campus (a.k.a., some place I had never been) that was at least fifteen minutes away. Then, I made the choice to check my e-mail; instead of just quickly scanning any unread messages, I felt it was appropriate to spend the next fifteen minutes at the computer. Next, after leaving myself absolutely zero room for error, I dashed off to the appointment (did I mention the room was filled with people from all over the country?) and got lost. As soon as I realized the client was upset, my first impulse was to blame Erin. Who was really at fault in this situation?

LIFE IS ALL ABOUT DECISIONS

You bought this book because at some level you felt that your life was incomplete. You made the purchase hoping that within these pages you would find a secret formula for more wealth, better relationships, greater fulfillment at work, and even better health. In other words, you are looking for different results than your current efforts are producing. I'm not suggesting that you're miserable; you are simply searching for something more.

I'd like to suggest that you consider the following diagram as you reflect on your dilemma.

RESULTS

↑

BEHAVIOR

↑

DECISIONS

You bought this book hoping to generate different results (money, happiness, etc.) in your life. In order to achieve those results, you realize that you must change your behavior (exceed expectations, be grateful, live in the moment, learn every day, etc.). What you may not realize is that in order for you to have improved results and better behavior, you need to make better decisions. You are a decision making machine from the minute you wake up in the morning until you drift off to sleep at night; these choices lead to changes in behavior that produce either good or bad results.

Take a look at your average day. Your alarm goes off at 5:30

A.M. because getting to work a little early helps you to get a head start on your day. When you hear that alarm, you can pop out of bed or hit the snooze button on your alarm clock. Either way, this decision will affect your morning, so do you get to work early and get a head start on your day or do you rush around all morning trying to beat traffic? At work, your assistant shows up fifteen minutes late for the fifth day in a row. You can chose to say something right now to make sure it doesn't happen again or you can ignore it because you hate confrontation.

Later in the day, you lose a customer because he claims business is down and the company can no longer afford your services. You can sulk in your office wondering if you can survive this recession or you can pick up the phone and do whatever it takes to get a new customer. After work, you walk into your house at 6 P.M. and your spouse wants to talk to you about some challenges he or she had during the day. Regardless of whether or not you are interested in hearing the story, you can pay close attention and empathize with his or her situation or turn on the TV, offering a half-hearted "Hmm" at the pauses in the conversation. As the day comes to a close, you have one final decision: do you go to bed at 10 P.M. or stay up to watch one more hour of TV? Guess what happens to your next day if you stay up too late?

As this example shows, your day (and mine) is filled with activity and circumstances; most importantly, your waking hours are filled with opportunities to make decisions. In his book, *The 8th Habit*, Steven Covey points out that our ability to thoughtfully make decisions throughout the day is what truly separates us from every other species on earth.

Covey argues that something happens to us every day. Our kids disobey, our clients get angry, we land a new prospect, we get a cold, etc. After each one of these circumstances (stimulus), we have the ability to respond. We can yell at our kids, cry about our clients, celebrate a new prospect, or stay in bed because we feel sick. Your response isn't what makes you special; it's your ability to respond. Covey points out, *"Between stimulus and response, there is a space. In that space lies our freedom and power to choose our response. In those choices lie our growth and our happiness."*[35]

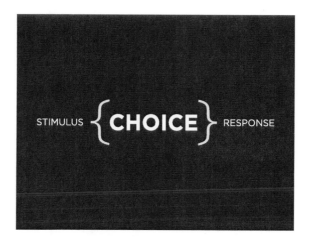

No matter what happens to us, we all have the ability to choose how we are going to respond and these choices (decisions) shape our lives. Often during my speeches, I ask the audience the following question: "Raise your hand if you earned exactly what you chose to earn during the previous twelve months." As you can imagine, not a hand is raised. I follow up by telling the people in the room that each of them earned *exactly what they chose* to earn during the previous twelve months. I assume that many members of the audience (and maybe even you) are thinking, "He just doesn't understand my business and how hard it's been during this recession."

Truth be told, your circumstances (recession, new competitor, etc.) don't matter. As M. Scott Peck points out in his bestseller *The Road Less Traveled*, "Life is difficult." We will all face difficult circumstances, and yes, some will be harder than others. However, we all have the ability to choose how we are going to respond to these circumstances, and as Dr. Covey reminds us, it is in these choices that lie our growth and our happiness.[36] The final strategy for living your extraordinary life is to take responsibility for your decisions and choose your future. Your life is truly what you make of it, no matter what challenges you face along the way.

WHY DO WE BLAME?

I am 100 percent certain that you didn't just finish the first portion of this chapter and exclaim to yourself, "This guy is brilliant. I never realized that there are consequences for my actions!" You were probably first taught this lesson as a small child when you learned that disobeying your parents had consequences. For example, I often tell (a.k.a., threaten) my children (ages seven and four) that "If you do this (ignore my request to put on your pajamas), then the consequence will be that (no stories before bed)." As you got older, the importance of taking responsibility was (hopefully) reinforced in school because studying was rewarded with better grades. After school you should have learned on the job that those individuals who worked harder and learned more were able to get a promotion and earn a better salary.

Intellectually speaking, you know that you are in control of your life and your efforts can shape your future. It's a fairly simple concept to grasp. But why, if it's so simple, do you (and me and just about everybody else) blame our clients, Congress, the media, our neighbors, the economy, etc., when things don't go our way? Unfortunately, the answer isn't that simple. In fact, it is very complex and different for every person. Here are a few of the fundamental reasons we tend to look outward instead of inward for solutions to our problems.

First, blaming outside circumstances (stimuli) makes us feel better. No one likes to look back at decisions they have made in life and admit they made a mistake (didn't study hard enough, said something offensive, etc.) because it makes us feel inadequate and causes emotional pain. At some level we are all programmed to avoid this pain and as a result we blame. This blaming lifts the hurt of past decisions which led to the bad results.

Prior to starting my own firm, I worked at a company that would have been a perfect case study for analyzing why a group of talented and driven people could allow themselves to become obsessed with blaming outside factors for their current circumstances. Each day, we would complain from the minute we walked in the building at 8 A.M. until we left in the evening. As ridiculous as this might sound, sometimes it seemed that the workday was less about delivering a product to the customer and more about who could come up with the most unique reason why our company would implode at any minute.

Looking back, I now realize that the reason we complained so much was because we were mad that we allowed ourselves to work at that type of company and complaining made us feel better about the choice we made to work there. Finally, I woke up one day (after three years of blaming our development staff, the CEO, and our gullible customers) and realized that I needed to make a decision; I could stop blaming the situation for my frustration or quit and do something different. I am still amazed that I allowed myself to blame others for three years just to feel better about my choices.

In addition to making us feel better, I believe that most people blame because it is easier and when difficult situations arise, most tend to try and find a quick solution that requires the least effort. For example, when I ask a room full of people why it is that they don't exercise, many find comfort in the "I don't have the time" answer. In reality, they have the exact same twenty-four hours in a day as everyone else. They chose the "time" excuse because it is easy and doesn't require them to carefully analyze their schedule and consider a thoughtful solution for getting in shape.

During the past two years, I have seen hundreds of professionals choose the "easy" solution by blaming the economy for their drop in sales and profits. Seldom do they look in the mirror and admit that their sales are down because they haven't chosen to respond to their difficult circumstances (increased pricing pressures, less demand, etc.) more effectively. I witnessed a refreshing exception to this rule when a close friend of mine, who owned a construction company, reflected back upon a rough 2009. Although his industry had absolutely collapsed during this recession, he indicated that the reason his company had seen a drop in sales was because he didn't respond to the downturn as quickly as he should have. He admitted, "As much as I would like to blame the economy, my company had a bad year because of me."

We blame because it makes us feel better and it is easier. But, how did we get this way in the first place? Take, for example, the company I discussed earlier in this chapter. I don't remember accepting a position at this company hoping to be surrounded by a group of people that complained all day long and I doubt my coworkers did either. Why did a group of young professionals decide that instead of taking responsibility and taking care of their customers, they would blame the management team for their current situation?

I believe that although we have had individuals (parents, teachers, coaches) who taught us to take responsibility for our lives, we are conditioned by our environment to blame others when something doesn't go right. And by "environment", I am primarily referring to the mass media. Because we live in a society that is bombarded with so much information, rarely do we take the time to carefully analyze a situation, instead relying on snippets of data otherwise known as sound bites. When a challenging situation arises, those involved realize they have to quickly and forcefully blame others or they will be held responsible. All of this finger pointing has created a culture where blaming others has become both expected and fully acceptable.

As I write this chapter, the country is in day fifty-four of the oil crisis in the Gulf of Mexico. It has turned into a nonstop blame fest, so much so that the cover of Time magazine features a bird that has been covered with oil and the following headline, "How to Clean Up this Mess – And Who's to Blame?" The governor of Louisiana, Bobby Jindal, is blaming BP (British Petroleum) and the federal government. The federal government (President Obama) is blaming BP and the past administration (George Bush). The Republicans are blaming President Obama, BP, and the federal government. I wonder if we would have this thing figured out if we focused as much energy on the solution as we did on making sure everyone knows it's the other guy's fault.

Perhaps the best example of this figure pointing (possibly of all time) is our country's reflection upon our financial system's meltdown, resulting in the worst recession since the Great Depression. It's absolutely critical to the financial future of our country and the world that we learn from our mistakes and prevent this from happening again. Unfortunately, all anyone wants to do is to blame everyone else. If all you did was observe this discussion in the media (which is what most people do), you would think the meltdown was nobody's fault.

So, there you have it. We tend to blame other people because it makes us feel better and it's easy. In addition, we live in a cultural environment that actually teaches us to blame others when a challenge arises in our lives that causes us pain. For many, it seems like taking responsibility for your life and your actions is so challenging that it isn't worth the effort. I think these people are wrong, and in the next section, I am going to show you why you can't live an extraordinary life without holding yourself accountable for choosing your future.

THE BENEFITS OF CHOICE

By now you have probably realized that I am a big fan of the simplest solution. As a result, once a prospect enters into my sales process I ask the person two simple questions. First, I ask him or her to fast forward to a time in the future and imagine that everything had gone perfectly in his or her business, association, management team, etc. After I have an understanding about where the person wants to go, I then follow up and ask if there are any current habits or behaviors that could keep him or her from getting there. If they can't identify one opportunity for improvement (time management, become a better leader, etc.), then I immediately conclude that the person wouldn't be a good fit for my services. These people either have achieved everything they have ever wanted or *don't believe an improvement in their behavior can improve their current circumstances.*

My experience has shown that if you don't believe that you have the ability to improve your situation by modifying your behavior, you will always blame outside circumstances when something goes wrong. These people go through life bouncing from situation to situation completely out of control. No matter what happens they feel like victims, completely unable to improve their life on their own. One of the most valuable benefits you receive from choosing your future is that you are able to maintain some control of your life.[37]

As I mentioned in chapter 2, over the past seven years, I have asked more than two hundred clients the following question: "What would your perfect life look like?" Not once has a business owner had a thoughtful response to this answer. Instead, after some rambling, they agree that it would be nice to have a house on the ocean and not have to work so much. The reason these business owners struggle so much with this question isn't because they aren't driven, talented, and resourceful; rather, it is because, at some level, they don't believe they are in charge of their future.

Once you truly understand that you have the ability to choose your responses to life's opportunities and challenges, you gain confidence in answering questions about your future. You realize that your extraordinary life isn't something that just happens to you; it is something that you design.

Let's look at how this change in viewpoint can transform someone's life. Imagine that you know a forty-year-old man named Gary who works in middle management for a large manufacturing company. His company has weathered the recession fairly well, but Gary hasn't seen a raise in pay in more than three years. In addition, he has been passed over for a promotion twice. Last year, Gary had a medical problem that increased his personal debt by more than five thousand dollars. At home Gary has two young children who stay at home with his wife, a former accountant. If you and Gary were hanging out, having a few beers, and discussing life, he would admit that he is extremely frustrated with his job, unhappy with his marriage, overwhelmed by his personal debt, tired of feeling out of shape, and positive that things won't change unless he wins the lottery.

Then, he reads a book which convinces him that regardless of the challenges he faces, he has the ability to choose how he responds to these difficulties. He recognizes that every day is filled with opportunities, and instead of being a victim, he wants to take control of his life. This paradigm shift completely changes the way he approaches every situation. Instead of hitting the snooze button five times when the alarm clock goes off because he dreads the upcoming day, Gary chooses to get up thirty minutes earlier than usual, stretches, and goes for a walk around the neighborhood. He convinces his wife that they need to gain control of their financial situation (to which she exclaims, "It's about time!") and they decide to attend a personal financial planning course at their church.

Next, Gary asks his boss if he could schedule a meeting to talk about his career. In this meeting, Gary gives his boss a clear image of what the perfect job would look like five years in the future and asks if this type of job exists at their company as well as any skills that he would need to acquire to land such a position. Finally, Gary schedules a babysitter (his parents) to watch the kids every Thursday night so that he and his wife can have a regular date night.

If you were to fast forward five years, what changes do you think you would see in Gary's life after he chose to take control? He may not be the CEO of his company, have ten million dollars in the bank, and have buns of steel, but don't you think he will see a significant improvement in his life simply because he chose to take 100 percent responsibility? He has shifted from being a victim with a terrible job, debt problems, and a lousy marriage to a driven individual who looks forward to the challenges and opportunities each day delivers. You can take your life from unhappy to extraordinary by making a simple choice. Take control of your life and choose your future.

The second important benefit you experience once you choose to take responsibility for every aspect of your life is the gift of a daily education. The minute you decide that your mistakes are a result of your choices, you begin to experience learning opportunities throughout each and every day. Without this perspective, you dismiss these opportunities as unfortunate circumstances that are outside of your control.

For example, I spend a lot time helping my clients improve their sales. In this role, I have frequent discussions with their sales teams in which we discuss wins and losses. Unfortunately, when analyzing their activity most salespeople will blame the loss on a client's ignorance, an unfair advantage held by a competitor, or their inferior product/service. Those excuses are almost never true. In fact, I tell every sales team I work with that if you have properly qualified the prospect (they are a good fit for your product/service and have the budget) you should expect to win the deal *every single time*. I tell them that if they don't win the deal every time it's because they didn't effectively execute the sales process. My point isn't to convince them that they should maintain a 100 percent conversation rate. Rather, I want them to recognize that each loss represents an opportunity to learn and improve.

If you blame outside circumstances for problems in your life, you will never learn. It is that simple. If you dropped a class because the teacher spoke with an accent, you may miss an opportunity to learn that you really struggle with a subject. If, after your third divorce, you believe that all women are "just plain crazy", you may miss a flaw in your personality. If you get fired by the sixth "idiot boss" in a row, you may miss a chance to learn how to upgrade your professional skill set. As we mentioned in chapter 5, constant improvement is a key ingredient for your extraordinary life. This improvement is impossible without taking responsibility for your own life and choosing your future.

This year, you will experience both good and bad circumstances. Regardless, as Dr. Covey pointed out, your happiness is a direct result of how you choose to respond to each one. Please note, as with the other strategies in this book, intellectually, this concept is easy to grasp. Making it a daily habit is much more difficult. In the next section, I will provide you with some simple tips for making it work.

PUTTING "CHOICE" INTO PRACTICE

It is highly likely that within the next twenty-four hours you will be faced with a situation that doesn't go as planned and you will be faced with the urge to blame someone or something else for the results. It may be a lost client, a prospect who says no, an angry wife, or a frustrated boss. Whatever it is, your gut will insist that this isn't your fault. It's in these situations that we need to ensure that taking responsibility becomes an unconscious habit. Here are a few uncomplicated strategies to help you put this into practice.

I take the first suggestion directly from John G. Miller's book, *The Question Behind the Question (QBQ) – Practicing Personal Accountability in Work and in Life.* In this short and easy read, Miller suggests that every single time you face a challenge, resist the urge to blame and instead ask the question behind the question. Before you begin to blame someone or something else for a bad circumstance ("Why didn't they call me?" or "Why is she always late?"), ask yourself if you could have done anything differently to improve the situation. He doesn't suggest blaming yourself; his recommendation is simply to take a second to reflect on your behavior before jumping to blame. For whatever reason, I find that this simple phrase has helped me to develop the habit of always taking personal responsibility for my life. For example, every time one of my clients decides to ignore my advice, I first wonder if I could have communicated it more effectively. So, the next time you are tempted to blame, simply ask yourself the question behind the question or "What could I have done differently?" The answer might be nothing, but I still recommend that you start with this question.

Before I provide the next tactic, I want you to imagine driving in your car on a busy road and you need to change lanes. In addition to checking your rear view mirror before switching lanes, you should also look over your shoulder or you might hit a car in your blind spot. No matter how self-aware you may become, just like your car, you have a blind spot. This blind spot is a personality flaw; for whatever reason you just don't see it. For many people, this blind spot is their inability to recognize when they are blaming others for their problems. As a result, I highly recommend that you ask others to look out for you. Give your friends, family (yes, even your spouse), and coworkers the permission to let you know when you drift into the blame game.

Finally, I find it valuable to set aside some time on a daily (at least weekly) basis to reflect upon your activity in the past. Similar to using a Gratitude Journal (chapter 5), I recommend that you keep a notebook that contains lessons you learn on a regular basis. Every morning I ask myself the following question, "If I could redo yesterday, what would I do differently?" This simple practice helps develop the habits of continuous improvement (chapter 6) and will help you take 100 percent responsibility for your behavior.

The road towards your extraordinary life is paved with learning opportunities. Make certain that you don't miss any of these by choosing to take responsibility for your life. This can be accomplished by asking the question behind the question, asking others to hold you accountable, and documenting what you've learned. As with everything, it all starts with a choice.

WHAT I REALLY WANT YOU TO REMEMBER...

1. Life is Full of Decisions – We are all decision making machines, from the minute we open our eyes until we go to bed. All personal growth starts by improving our ability to effectively analyze data and make better decisions.

2. It's Your Choice – Every single day we will be faced with both positive and negative circumstances. Our success, both personally and professionally, is a direct result of the way in which we choose to respond to these circumstances.

3. The Blame Game – The average human being (you and me included) tends to blame others when things don't go his or her way. Unfortunately, our culture reinforces and actually rewards this behavior.

4. Take the Road Less Traveled – Taking responsibility for your actions is difficult, however it's worth it. There are many valuable benefits including:
- Control of your life
- Daily opportunities to learn and improve

5. Practice – Just about everyone around you succumbs to blaming outside circumstances for the challenges they face. These simple tactics will help you to make choosing your future a habit:
- Ask the question behind the question
- Permit others to hold you accountable
- Document what you learn

CHAPTER 9
MAKE IT HAPPEN

*"Motivation is what gets you started.
Habit is what keeps you going."*

Jim Rohn
Author and speaker

So there you have it; five simple strategies for helping you achieve your extraordinary life. As you begin the final chapter, I have some good news and some bad news. First, the good news–I guarantee that turning these simple strategies into habits will help you to achieve your extraordinary life. Now, the bad news–books don't work, people do.

In the first few chapters of this book, I discussed the concept that we already know what to do but for a variety of reasons don't do it. Thus, I believe that "books don't work, people do." In other words, no matter how much you enjoyed these nine chapters, no matter how many times you underlined passages, and no matter how often you told your friends about the concept you just learned, this book will not change your life. Only *you* can change your life. Books can inspire you and provide the knowledge to change your life, but *nothing happens unless you make it happen.*

For example, consider a handful of powerful lessons that have been taught by some of the greatest teachers of all time.

1. *Think and Grow Rich* (Napoleon Hill) – In 1937, Napoleon Hill pointed out that one of "the most common causes of failure is quitting when one is overtaken by temporary defeat."[38]
2. *The Power of Positive Thinking* (Norman Vincent Peale) – More than fifty years ago, Peale taught the world that in order to enjoy success, you need to expect the best instead of the worst; this simple mindset can help you overcome just about any obstacle.
3. *The Seven Habits of Highly Effective People* (Dr. Steven Covey) – In one of my personal favorites, Dr. Covey suggests that before you begin any journey, you must "begin with the end in mind." In other words, setting clear goals can help ensure your success.

4. *The E-Myth* (Michael Gerber) – By sharing a simple story about a small business owner/pie maker named Sarah, Gerber demonstrates how entrepreneurs struggle to grow profitably without building simple processes in their company.

5. *One Minute Manager* (Ken Blanchard) – In this short and simple book, Blanchard teaches a three-step process for getting the most out of your people – set clear expectations, praise their accomplishments, and hold them accountable when they fall short.

I picked these five by glancing at my bookshelf for five minutes. I could have easily added another ten or twenty whose titles many would recognize. Over the past seventy years, there have been hundreds (if not thousands) of great books that have each taught many valuable lessons. These books have sold millions of copies worldwide and have been translated into dozens of languages. In other words, we know exactly what to do, because we bought the books. However, I know very few people who have implemented any of these simple lessons.

At this point you are probably beginning to wonder, why should I keep reading all of these books and learning all of this new stuff if I am not going to change my behavior? A student of mine shared this viewpoint in class the other day when he exclaimed, "I have taken the Dale Carnegie course, listened to all of the CDs, and read all of the books, but I still don't practice the necessary behavior to sell!" Don't despair: In this last chapter, I will teach you how to take what you've learned in this book and utilize it to make a lasting change in your behavior. In addition, I will provide you with some simple rules for getting the most out of every book you read and workshop you attend. But I will warn you first, it's not going to be easy.

IT'S CALLED WORK FOR A REASON

Back in chapter 3, I told you that I believe, intellectually speaking, changing a behavior is simple; actually changing that behavior is hard. There are three simple reasons why people don't change:

- The pain associated with the current behavior isn't strong enough.
- We only change behavior when there is instant gratification.
- It's difficult to make an emotional connection with the reward for change.

In other words, even though these five strategies are simple to grasp and putting them into practice should be easy, it isn't. Here's where I will truly break from many of the personal growth books that you have read in the past. There isn't a "quick fix" for building an extraordinary life because making these habits part of your everyday routine isn't going to be easy. It's called work for a reason.

Unfortunately, as I have mentioned many times throughout this book, unless an activity delivers an immediate result, most of us aren't interested in hard work. I was reminded of this truth last year when a dear friend of mine asked me to participate in a program that mentors at-risk high school students. A group of professionals (accountants, lawyers, bankers, me) were asked to spend a semester with a handful of high school seniors who were in need of some inspiration. We had a great two hour orientation session with the leader of the program and each week he provided us with a concise curriculum to guide our work with the students.

Mr. "Know it All" (me) ignored all of this guidance and decided to try his own approach.[39] I brought a copy of one of my favorite books, *The Magic of Thinking Big*, by Joseph Schwartz, and brought it to one of our sessions. I told my students that we would take time to review these principles in each of our meetings together and added the following challenge: if they shared this book, which was less than two hundred pages, and read every chapter by the end of the semester, I would give each of them one hundred fifty dollars in cash. (Keep in mind that one hundred fifty dollars to a high school senior is big money.)

In addition, I challenged each of the four students to read this book once a month for the next five years. I promised to write each of them a check for fifty thousand dollars if they read this book monthly for the next five years and didn't out-achieve every one of their peers. Before anyone could say, "You are full of it", I looked each of them in the eye and promised to document the agreement in writing. At the end of the semester, the pitiful results were in—one student had read a quarter of the book, while the other three complained they didn't "have the time" to even get started. The worst part of this story is that I am not even sure if I blame the kids because they are being shaped by a society that encourages them to avoid hard work at all costs in favor of Facebook, Twitter, text messages, and other media that promise instant gratification.

The same is true for all of us. We are convinced that life should be easy, fun, and provide non-stop entertainment; this notion is reinforced everywhere you look. As we discussed in chapter 3, not only do we look for the easy solution, we absolutely expect it. Please note, I am not saying that we don't work hard; even with the advent of technology, we still work a lot. What I am saying is that we aren't committed to dedicating our efforts towards something that doesn't provide an immediate result. In other words, we will work a twelve-hour day on a bunch of individual projects, frequently switching to something new when we get bored, but we won't dedicate the hours necessary to develop a new habit.

As a result, every year thousands of books are published, workshops are delivered, and podcasts are recorded that promise a quick and easy solution to everything from credit card debt to a flat stomach. The most interesting thing about all of this content is that it is virtually identical from year to year. We have all of the answers, but because we don't discipline ourselves to delay gratification for more than twenty-seven minutes we get distracted halfway through the book, workshop, or podcast. Thus, we go back to our old habit and end up buying the next self-help book promising a quick fix.

Here's a great story illustrating this challenge. I know a guy who is 6 feet 5 inches, skinny, really good looking (a little bald on top), and who has had back problems his entire life. Every single time back pain settles in, he moans for a few days until he decides to visit a doctor. The doctor (usually a physical therapist) provides him with a packet of information containing a handful of simple stretches that should eliminate back pain if done regularly (twenty minutes a day, three to four days a week). This handsome and otherwise intelligent young man does these exercises for about three weeks and then concludes that the back problem is cured. But guess what always happens? That's right, the back pain returns. This knucklehead knows exactly what to do but struggles to commit to a simple and easy regimen of stretching, even though the results (a healthy back) are virtually guaranteed.[40]

The good news is that you are only five simple strategies away from living your extraordinary life. The bad news is that "to know and not to do is really not to know." However, you are in luck. I am committed to helping you turn these tactics into habits that will change the way you live. This is not just another resource that provides some interesting insights. It is a collection of common sense ideas including a practical plan that leads to a new you. But, as I said before, it won't be easy. It's called work for a reason.

THE PLAN

Talk, as they say, is cheap. The unfortunate truth is that if you don't make at least one slight change in your behavior after reading this book, then it will have been a waste of your time and money. So, I have detailed a plan that, if followed, will lead to change every single time. Before I detail the plan, I want to discuss The Four Stages of Learning Model,[41] which I believe provides the best framework for understanding the development of a new habit. This model suggests that we go through four stages of learning before a skill becomes routine. Below, I have defined each stage and included a corresponding example that, unfortunately, applies to me.

Unconsciously Incompetent – In this first stage you don't recognize that you have a deficiency or a need to improve a skill and, as a result, you make no effort to do so. For example, in social situations you rarely pay complete attention to the person who is talking, allowing your attention to wander throughout the conversation. It is apparent to everyone else and is extremely rude.

Consciously Incompetent–You enter this stage once someone informs you of your deficiency and you realize you have an issue that needs to be addressed. In these social situations you realize that you don't pay attention to the current conversation, but you haven't yet developed the skill of blocking outside distractions and giving the person the courtesy of being completely present.

Consciously Competent – After some practice you eventually develop the skill, but it requires conscious effort to regularly exercise your new ability. Finally, people can stand to be around you in social situations because you listen intently to what they are saying and ignore interruptions.

Unconsciously Competent – The new skill becomes a habit as soon as it simply happens without giving it any conscious or focused thought. Examples include driving, running, or brushing your teeth. Believe it or not, giving someone else your full attention at a party or networking event can become second nature.

The Four Stages of Learning Model clearly illustrates that through conscious effort we can take a skill and turn it into a habit. The goal for this book's final chapter is twofold: First, I will teach you a set of simple tactics that will help you move from unconscious incompetence to unconscious competence with each of the five strategies in this book. Second, I will convince you that no matter how difficult it may be, this journey is worth the effort.

It's hard to imagine that at some point in your life you haven't been exposed to each of the concepts in this book. I very much doubt that I am the first person to suggest that you need to live in the moment, exceed expectations, live gratefully, improve every day, and take 100 percent responsibility for your life. As a result, it is reasonable to argue that you didn't begin this journey unconsciously incompetent. Rather, you have known about these ideas but have not practiced them in your life, making you consciously incompetent. Unfortunately, as it relates to these simple personal development habits, most people spend the majority of their time consciously incompetent. You are a few pages away from no longer being considered one of those people. Stay with me, you won't be sorry.

ONE AT A TIME

Early in my coaching career, I had a client who was interested in buying a business that was complementary to their current offerings. After analyzing the opportunity, I concluded that it had all of the ingredients to be successful, it was in a growing market, had decent margins and a good brand name. However, I heavily advised my client not to move forward with the deal at the time.

The reason I recommended they pass was that they had yet to come even close to mastering the current markets they served. I felt strongly that adding a new business to the current mix of challenges was not worth the risk. They ignored my advice and bought the company. Less than two years later, they shut it down and decided to focus back on their core business. Unfortunately, this failed distraction cost them nearly five hundred thousand dollars not to mention an unbelievable amount of stress and frustration.

Most people fail when they try to change their behavior or develop a habit because they attempt to work on more than one at a time. Developing or changing a habit is extremely difficult work, and success requires focus and concentration. You can't lose weight and quit smoking at the same time, it's too difficult. Nor can you focus on more than one of the strategies in this book and hope to be victorious. This truth is especially relevant in today's modern society because distractions interrupt our every thought. As a result, I want you to work on one strategy at a time.

Now, it's time to choose your first strategy; this choice will set the stage for the rest of this journey. This first strategy is important because you need a running start if you intend on being successful at changing a lifetime of behavior. In other words, I want you to pick a strategy that will help you to build momentum. I would advise that you choose the habit you believe will result in the most important and positive impact in your life. The following questions will help you make this decision.

1. What is the biggest challenge you are experiencing in your professional and personal life (that is the result of your behavior)?
2. What are the personal and professional results of this challenge?

3. Which of the five strategies will most effectively address this challenge?

Consider the following example: You are the CEO of a manufacturing company and your sales have been declining for more than two years. Your best customers are unhappy and many are considering switching to your competition. In addition, company morale is at an all-time low and the board of directors is demanding an immediate improvement. Your job is definitely on the line. Unfortunately, the situation is creating so much stress in your life that you bring it home with you to your family. As soon as you walk in the door each evening, you retreat to your office and begin checking e-mail. The brief moments during which you break from work and spend time with your family are filled with tense short conversations. The board is frustrated, your employees are unhappy, and you haven't had a pleasant conversation with your kids in months. Something has to change.

The CEO could answer the above questions in the following manner:

1. **What is the biggest challenge you are experiencing in your professional and personal life (that is the result of your behavior)?**
   The biggest challenge is my inability to grow the sales in my company.

2. **What are the personal and professional results of this challenge?**
   This inability has placed my job in jeopardy and caused serious damage to the relationship I have with my family.

3. **Which of the five strategies will most effectively address this challenge?**

There is no easy solution to this problem. Ultimately, I need to execute many tactics to get our sales back on track. However, I believe that it makes the most sense for me to initially focus on exceeding expectations. Our inability to exceed the expectations of our clients has led to our drop in revenue. This has hurt morale and led me to lose sight of my employees' expectations. Worst of all, I take my work stress home and don't even come close to meeting the expectations of my family, much less exceeding them.

Obviously, this isn't an exact science. You could have probably picked another of the five strategies and gotten a satisfactory result. Remember, the goal of this first exercise is to gain some momentum and the best way to do so is to get a win under your belt. You need to see some results; if you don't, there is no way you will move on to the second strategy. How many times have you started a project only to give up after it became somewhat difficult? Ironically enough, most people quit right before they are about to begin to have some success. If you're interested in using what you've learned to help you live an extraordinary life, focus on one strategy at a time.

Before we move on, take a second and answer these questions for yourself.

What is the biggest challenge you are experiencing in your professional and personal life (that is the result of your behavior)?

What are the personal and professional results of this challenge?

```



```

Which of the five strategies will most effectively address this challenge?

```



```

Now that you have chosen a strategy, here is a simple four step process that will ensure you are successful.

STEP #1 — CREATE VISUAL REMINDERS

In Chapter 11 of his bestselling book, *The Success Principles* (my favorite book of all time), Jack Canfield suggests that you "See what you want and get what you see." Canfield argues that the brain thinks in pictures, and if we create a vivid illustration of what it is that we want to achieve, our brain will figure out how to get us there. He tells a story about the actor Jim Carrey, who uses the power of visualization to help him achieve his goals. Before Carrey became a famous movie star, he was an unknown comedian from Canada. However, Carrey knew that he wanted to be a highly paid actor and decided to write a check to himself for twenty million dollars—with the phrase "for services rendered" in the memo line—in order to give himself daily reminders of the goals he wished to achieve.

After years of climbing the ranks in Hollywood, in 1996 Carrey was cast in a role for a dark comedy, *The Cable Guy*. His salary for the film: twenty million dollars.

I recommend that you follow Canfield's guidance and create a visual that helps you focus on one of the five strategies in this book or you will easily get distracted. As soon you put this book down, the outside world will begin its nonstop competition for your attention (in the form of e-mail, phone call, text message, television show or Internet blog post). If you don't have something to remind you what's important, you will forget all about this book and its message. We've all read a "life-changing book" only to forget the title, author's name, and central message just days after completion. A visual tool will help ensure this doesn't happen again.

In case you're one of those people who, like me, lack the creativity to develop a really great visual, let me provide a little guidance. First, I would simply start with the phrase that reflects the strategy you are going to work on first ("Exceed Expectations," "Be Grateful," "Learn," "Take 100% Responsibility," and "Live in the Moment"). Write down the phrase on a piece of paper and place it somewhere you look at throughout the day – on your mirror, phone, computer, etc. Here are a few examples.

- *Today, I am completely committed to exceeding the expectations of my clients, my employees and my family!*
- *Today, I will focus on all of the blessings that I have been provided including a healthy body, a loving family, wonderful friends and a satisfying career.*
- *Today, I will choose to live in each moment and work on keeping my mind from drifting to the past or the future.*

Next, pick a simple visual that represents a positive change you will see in your life after you have successfully implemented (a.k.a., become consciously competent) this strategy. For example, our CEO might create a letter from the board of directors congratulating him on turning the company around. Or, he might also consider finding a picture from a resort that he hopes to take his family to once things turn around. Regardless of the visual chosen, like the phrase, it must be placed in a prominent position you will refer to often. The best visual reminder in the world does no good in a binder sitting on your bookshelf.

I recommend that you practice writing down a phrase in the space below.

STEP #2 — MAP OUT YOUR DAY

My clients often tell me, "CJ, your coaching makes a ton of sense until I have my first crisis of the day," or "I can't take the time out of my schedule to develop these habits, I'm too busy." In other words, anyone can develop a new habit in a vacuum with no outside interference. Because none of us has the luxury of living in a distraction-free environment, we need to have a proactive approach towards developing these habits instead of just sitting back and waiting to see what happens.

Taking a "proactive approach" can mean a lot of different things to a lot of different people. For the purposes of this discussion (and just about every discussion), I would like to make it as simple as possible. Here's how I recommend that you plan for your day. Take five minutes in the morning (before you have checked your e-mail and voice-mail) and think about your day, asking yourself the following questions:

1. What appointments are on my schedule for today? How can this habit (exceeding expectations, being grateful, etc.) play a part in these meetings?

2. When do I feel stress during the day? How can this habit (exceeding expectations, being grateful, etc.) help deal with this stress?

3. What are the most important goals I want to achieve during the day? How can this habit (exceeding expectations, being grateful, etc.) help me to achieve these goals?

I realize that it might be extremely difficult to predict what's going to happen during a typical day. You argue that many things will pop up that are absolutely impossible to plan for at 7:30 A.M. I understand and agree with you. These three questions are designed to help you prepare for those activities that you know will be taking place. You can't predict everything, but you need to plan for those items that are unlikely to change. Let's again look at our CEO and see how this might apply to his day.

1. What appointments are on my schedule for today? How can this habit (exceeding expectations, being grateful, etc.) play a part in these meetings?

Today, I have three meetings. One meeting is with our largest customer (they aren't exactly happy with our performance), another is a phone call with the board, and the last meeting is, a performance review with my VP of operations. Prior to each meeting, I will jot down a list of exactly what I believe the expectations are for each of the individuals I will deal with in these meetings today. At the beginning of each meeting, I will confirm these expectations with the participants. Finally, I will make a commitment to each one to meet these expectations within an agreed upon time frame.

2. **When do I feel stress during the day? How can this habit (exceeding expectations, being grateful, etc.) help deal with this stress?**

   I feel stress throughout the entire day. However, for whatever reason, I feel the most stress when I am driving home at the end of the day and this stress pours over into my family life. Today, on the way home, I will remind myself that my family has expectations of me and that no matter what happened during my day, they expect me to be a great dad and spouse. Then, upon my arrival, I will focus exclusively on exceeding these expectations.

3. **What are the most important goals I want to achieve during the day? How can this habit (exceeding expectations, being grateful, etc.) help me to achieve these goals?**

   After thinking through my day, I realize that three absolutely critical objectives rise above the rest of my to-do's – repair the relationship with our largest client, assure the board that I have a solid plan for the next ninety days, and reset expectations with the leader of our operations team. It's clear to me that if I do a great job at setting and exceeding expectations in each of my meetings today, it will increase the likelihood that I will achieve each of these goals.

In space below, take a few minutes to document how you expect today (or tomorrow) to unfold.

What appointments are on my schedule for today? How can this habit (exceeding expectations, being grateful, etc.) play a part in these meetings?

When do I feel stress during the day? How can this habit (exceeding expectations, being grateful, etc.) help deal with this stress?

What are the most important goals I want to achieve during the day? How can this habit (exceeding expectations, being grateful, etc.) help me to achieve these goals?

STEP #3 — FIND SOME ACCOUNTABILITY

For the past three years I have been one of those people who "think about writing a book." Whenever anyone asks how I am doing, I tell them that work is fine, the kids are great, and I am considering many topics for my first book. At a Christmas party last December, I was again having this conversation with a friend of mine, Josh, who had heard this story many times before. After a couple of drinks, Josh looks at me and jokingly points out, "CJ, you are never going to write this book; *please* stop talking about it." Of course I couldn't let someone call me out like that at a Christmas party; moments later I announced to the crowd that not only would I write a book in 2010, but I would have the first draft complete by June 30, 2010. And, because I had consumed two cold, frosty beverages instead of just one, I told the group of people standing near Josh and me that if I didn't complete by this date (June 30, 2010) I would get a permanent tattoo of Josh on my right bicep. (And here I sit on June 27th, putting together the final chapter.)

This journey you are about to take is going to be difficult. There will be many times when you are tempted to quit because it is hard and you can't see the immediate benefits of your efforts. One of the best ways to ensure that you don't give up is to engage someone else in your journey because your chances of achieving anything difficult are greatly increased if you have someone holding you accountable. Seldom do you hear a story about a successful person overcoming difficult odds without the assistance of a coach, mentor, or friend to keep them focused on the ultimate objective.

I have seen the power of accountability at work for the past seven years. Every day I speak to at least one client who has veered off the path that they know will ultimately lead to success. As their coach, I remind them of the value of their future achievements and the progress that they have already made. Rarely do I bring a groundbreaking insight to the table. Rather, I provide the third party voice of reason that can see through the clutter and bring some clarity to the situation. You will need the same clarity on your journey.

The person you choose to help you stay focused on one of these habits doesn't need to be a paid professional. All you need is a friend, coworker, or family member who will agree to hold you accountable as you work on becoming consciously competent with each of these habits. Holding someone accountable isn't rocket science, but it does require two extremely important factors – honesty and consistency.

Whomever you chose to help you stay focused on what you are trying to accomplish must agree to give you honest feedback. It's easy to tell someone what he or she wants to hear, but it can be very difficult to tell that person the truth. For example, the CEO in our previous examples can't choose a person (e.g., an employee who is terrified of losing his or her job) who provides dishonest criticism. If the CEO does a poor job of exceeding the expectations of a client, prospect, or their staff, the CEO will need someone to let him or her know that he or she missed the mark.

Next, sporadically holding someone accountable doesn't work because if you don't know when to expect accountability, you will tend to ignore it altogether. I have had many clients over the years cancel our meetings because they were "too busy" only to have my effectiveness as their coach decrease over time. Believe it or not, we all crave predictability and consistency. The best way to ensure that you stay focused on developing the habit in question is to have someone hold you accountable on a regular basis. And, by regular, I mean that this individual touches base with you on (at least) a weekly basis.

Again, imagine that you are the CEO and have decided that it is time to begin working on the habit of exceeding expectations.

I would advise you to identify a trusted friend who you respect to hold you accountable because all of your employees report to you and your wife isn't your biggest fan at the moment. You want to find someone who will provide you with unemotional and honest feedback about your performance. Next, I would recommend that you talk to this person on a weekly basis and have them ask you the following questions:

1. **Over the past seven days, did you make an effort to exceed the expectations of your family, friends, employees, prospects, and clients?**

2. **Give me some examples where you did a really great job of exceeding expectations.**

3. **Tell me about some instances where you didn't do so well? Why do you think you struggled with these circumstances? How will you do better in the future?**

4. **Are you still committed to making this change in behavior? Why?**

That's it. The conversation doesn't need to last more than fifteen minutes. As the CEO, you will be amazed at how the anticipation of this brief weekly conversation will affect your decision making. There will be times when you are tempted to scrap the whole "exceeding expectations" habit for at least the rest of the day. Then, you will remember that someone is going to hold you accountable and you will recommit to the habit.

If you're ready to make the change, having someone whom you trust to be honest and hold you accountable on a regular basis is critical to your success. If you could do it on your own, chances are you would have done it already.

Here, list the names of three individuals who you think might be able to do a good job of holding you accountable.

1. _____

2. _____

3. _____

STEP # 4 — REFLECT

When your accountability partner begins to run through their questions, I want you to be prepared to answer. A conversation filled with "I'm not sure," or "I think I did okay," won't do you very much good. You need to be prepared with some detailed examples of your successes and challenges because you will have both. In order to do this, I want to remind you about the importance of reflection that we discussed in chapter 6.

From the moment you open your eyes in the morning until you drift off to sleep in the evening, you will be bombarded with information. It's critical that you take a pause from this overload from time to time and ask yourself, "What can I learn from what just happened?" If you don't, you'll always feel a little overwhelmed and declare, "I'm too busy to slow down and develop any new habits." You need to reflect.

As we discussed, reflection is a simple concept that requires very little effort to effectively execute. However, as with everything, it does require the discipline to carry out an activity that will not generate an immediate result. Here's the activity I advise: Get yourself a leather bound journal that costs more than three dollars. As silly as this sounds, the more expensive this journal, the more you will value its contents. Do not expect this exercise to work if you grab a yellow note pad from the supply closet. Next, set aside ten to fifteen minutes each day to reflect on your behavior. The best way to do this is to ask the questions you will be hearing from your accountability partner and document your honest answers. It really is that easy. Don't over-think it.

Before you move on to the next section, please take a minute and practice reflection. All you need to do is to write down one important lesson you learned from today as it relates to the habit you are working on at the moment.

28 DAYS

At this point, you should be ready to ask the following question, "How do I know that I have become consciously competent?" In other words, when do you know that you have mastered the new habit so that you can move on to the next one? This simple answer is that you will never master this habit. Even though you will learn and improve in each of these areas, you will never reach a point at which you can't improve. One of my favorite authors, Daniel Pink, discusses the concept of mastery in his new book,

Drive, arguing, "You can approach it. You can home in on it. You can get really, really close to it. But like Cezanne, you can never touch it. Mastery is impossible to realize fully."[42]

Even if you become unconsciously competent with each of these habits, there will still be room to get better. Can you imagine, always being grateful for what you have been given and exceeding expectations at all times? Just because you can't completely master each of these habits doesn't mean that you shouldn't try. As with any goal, the real reward isn't the achievement of your objective, but rather the person you become along the journey. And as I said in the first chapter of this book, you are just beginning your journey towards an extraordinary life.

Having said all of that, I want to provide you with a little more guidance than just saying, "You can never master anything. By the way, good luck on your journey!" I want to give you with a hard and fast timeline for making these habits part of your life. Focus on one habit for four weeks (twenty-eight days) and then switch to a new one, regardless of the progress you've made. During that twenty-eight day period, commit to the tactics we have discussed in this chapter (plan your day, visualization, accountability, reflections), and at the end of the phase, reflect on how you have done and move on.

It is unlikely (in fact, impossible) that at the end of this time period you will have become unconsciously competent with any of these strategies. That's okay; remember, this is a journey, not a destination. What I can guarantee you is that if you follow these guidelines and stay focused on each of these habits for twenty-eight days, you will become consciously competent with each one. They may not become a habit like brushing your teeth or driving a car, but you will consider each one as you make decisions throughout your day. In other words, they will become part of how you process information in the future, and this simple change will help you live your extraordinary life.

CONCLUSION

So, here you go again. You reached the end of another book (It could have been an audio CD or workshop) that provided some great ideas which could change your life. The million dollar question is (and has always been), "What do I do with what I've learned?" As with everything in life, it's your choice.

You can close this book, place it back on your shelf and hope/pray that you will remember its lessons in 48 hours. Or, maybe it's time to try a different approach. Maybe this time you should consider keeping this book on your desk until you actually see some changes in your behavior. If you chose this I option, I have some simple and practical advice that will help you succeed. Here's how it works:

1. Go and buy yourself a desktop calendar that has a page for each day of the year. Visit *www.calendars.com* to choose from hundreds.
2. Find today's date and write the name of the strategy you want to work on first at the top of this page and the next 27 pages.
3. Once you have completed 28 days, move to the next strategy and repeat.

I can't guarantee that 5 months from now you will be a millionaire, live in a mansion, and have rock hard abs or even a full head of hair. However, I will promise that the simple practice of focusing on these strategies for an extended period of time will change your behavior. The choice is clear, continue your current behavior and expect different results or do something different. Choose wisely.

1   Covey, Stephen, *The Seven Habits of Highly Effective People* (Habit #1 – Begin with the End in Mind).

2   Dr Greg P. Sipes - Ph.D., Sc.D., Clinical Psychologist, Senior Partner, Indiana Health Group, Inc. Founder, nextVoice, LLC.

3   The Bible - Matthew 7:12.

4   Covey, Stephen – *The Eighth Habit*, p 274.

5   The Haiti Micah Project - *http://www.haiti-micah.org/haiti-facts.html*.

6   "Even before deadly quake, Haiti's situation was dire." – DW.DE- January, 14, 2010.

7   Poverty Facts and Statistics – *www.globalissues.org*.

8   US Hunger Facts – *www.bread.org*
    "Millions More Thrust Into Poverty", Carol Morello and Dan Keating, *The Washington Post*.

9   Ibid.

10 Ibid.

11 Ibid.

12 Ibid.

13 Lindstrom, Martin - Buyology.

14 I have yet to fully embrace this concept. While I know it to be the right way to live, I find it hard to break my old way of thinking that the key to the extraordinary life is through acquisition and accumulation.

15 This study was completed by Robert A Emmons, University of California – Davis and Michael E. McCullough, University of Miami. Their study was later turned into a book titled *The Psychology of Gratitude*.

16 See "Highlights from the research Project on Gratitude and Thankfulness" - *http://psychology.ucdavis.edu/labs/emmons*.

17 For the full study visit - *http://www.oecd.org/document/11/0,3343, en_2649_34447_44981579_1_1_1_1,00.html*.

18 Information was taken from *http://www.faireconomy.org/files/GD_10_Chairs_ and_Charts.pdf*.

19 Ibid.

20 Bureau of Labor Statistics – Current Population Survey, September 2008.

21 *Patterns on Household Charitable Giving* by Income Group, 2005 – The Center on Philanthropy at Indiana University.

22 Ibid.

23 Ibid.

24 Ibid.

25 Source - comScore.

26 Ibid.

27 Imai, Masaaki (1986). *Kaizen: The Key to Japan's Competitive Success*. New York, NY, USA: Random House.

28 Internet 2010: Bots, Blogs and News Aggregators (White Paper) – Marcus P Zillman.

29 The Bible – Matthew 6:34.

30 Eckhart Tolle, *The Power of Now*, p 49.

31 Ibid, p 48.

32 Ibid, p 49.

33 "Hi-tech is turning us all into time-wasters - Mobile phones and emails are triggering the 'distraction' part of the brain." – Day, Michael – *The Observer*, July 20, 2008.

34 "Cognitive Control in Media Multitaskers." By Eyal Ophira, Clifford Nass, and Anthony D. Wagner. *Proceedings of the National Academy of Sciences*, Vol. 106 No. 33, August 25, 2009.

35 Covey, Stephen – *The Eighth Habit*, p 42.

36 Ibid.

37 I should note that I am a Christian and believe that ultimately the God I believe in is running the show. However, He has given me free will and expects me to take responsibility for my actions. In other words, he knows where I am going, but also recognizes I can chose my future.

38 Napoleon Hill, *Think and Grow Rich* – p 5.

39 I don't recommend ignoring the advice of these underpaid professionals unless you know more than they do, which I don't.

40 Obviously, this handsome man is me. I use the term struggled (past tense) because I did eventually develop this habit. But, it was only after I pulled out my "back pain" folder from a filing cabinet one year and noticed 4 packets of the same back stretches.

41 The origin of this model is Abraham Maslow.

42 Pink, Daniel - *Drive*, p 127.

ABOUT THE AUTHOR

CJ McClanahan is the founder and president of reachmore, a leadership training and consulting firm. He writes a column on leadership for the *Indianapolis Business Journal* and hosted central Indiana's premiere radio program for entrepreneurs - Lets' Talk Business. Over the past five years, CJ has spoken to thousands of professionals and has helped more than 250 business owners and corporate management teams achieve record sales and profits.

CJ is an avid reader and admits to being in a much better mood when the Nebraska Cornhuskers football team is ranked in the top 10. His greatest treasure continues to be his wife and two kids whom he lives with in Indianapolis, IN.